# Endorsements

I love this book! My friend Scott Tavolacci has given us a comprehensive approach to building God's kingdom on earth, as it is in heaven. *Kingdom Master Builders* will bring you into God's revelation of who God entrusts with His master plan for changing the world. Scott focuses on the attributes and character of heaven's ambassadors. This book is full of insights you may have never considered before. Take the step of becoming one of the *Kingdom Master Builders* in these last days! This book can change your life and change the planet!

**— Brian Simmons**
The Passion Translation Project
Passionandfire.com, ThePassiontranslation.com

Scott Tavolacci uses his skill as a storyteller to open our understanding to the kingdom of our Lord Jesus. Like binoculars, his teaching gift brings kingdom truths up close where they're more easily seen and understood. Come to the door and take hold of these kingdom keys!

**— Bob Sorge**
Author
Bobsorge.com

If there's a better, more comprehensive, well written, more informative, more revelatory, more biblically sound book about the kingdom of God, I don't know about it. This fact-filled and insightful book will genuinely inform you and excite you about the amazing kingdom of God! Every Bible-believing Christian should devour and digest every page. It is a "must read" for each citizen of the kingdom. Simply put, it's by far the best book on the subject that I've read. Wow! Good job, Scott!

**— Dennis Cramer**
Teacher/Prophet, Dennis Cramer Ministries
Denniscramer.com

This new book by my dear lifelong friend Scott Tavolacci, is indeed a *master*piece! It is a powerful biblical treatise on the kind of leadership that our world so desperately needs today, most importantly among those in authority roles in the church. With the brushes of scripture, Scott paints a clear, brilliant picture of what authentic spiritual authority is supposed to look like. In deep contrast to the secular tenets of our modern "culture of self," which preaches self-promotion and self-sufficiency as the sure road to success, we hear the call of Jesus to lead with humility, love, and sacrifice. The Apostle Paul echoed that call, urging us on as master builders, who advance the kingdom of God just as the Master did. Next-generation leaders need to read this book, study its content, and absorb it into their expressions of ministry. It is chock full of revelation and instructions for application.

**— Apostle Kathy Bichsel**
Kathy Bichsel Ministries
www.kathybichsel.com

# KINGDOM MASTER BUILDERS

A Revelation about Kingdom
Leadership and Authority

Scott J. Tavolacci

*Kingdom Master Builders: A Revelation about Kingdom Leadership and Authority*

Copyright © 2019 by Scott Tavolacci
Published by Kingdom Master Builders
www.kingdommasterbuilders.com

Unless otherwise notes, all scripture quotations are taken from the NEW AMERICAN STANDARD BIBLE®, Copyright © 1960,1962,1963,1968,1971,1972,1973,1975,1977,1995 by The Lockman Foundation. Used by permission.

All scripture quotations marked KJV are taken from the King James Version of the Bible. Public domain in the USA.

Scripture quotations marked MSG are taken from THE MESSAGE, copyright © 1993, 2002, 2018 by Eugene H. Peterson. Used by permission of NavPress. All rights reserved. Represented by Tyndale House Publishers, Inc.

Scripture quotations marked NLT are taken from the Holy Bible, New Living Translation, copyright © 1996, 2004, 2015 by Tyndale House Foundation. Used by permission of Tyndale House Publishers, Inc., Carol Stream, Illinois 60188. All rights reserved.

Note: all emphasis in scripture quotations is the author's own.

ISBN: 978-1-7340053-2-5 (Print)
     978-1-7340053-3-2 (Digital)

Printed in the USA

# CONTENTS

| | |
|---|---|
| FOREWORD | 7 |
| **PART 1: INTRODUCTION TO THE KINGDOM OF GOD** | **9** |
| INTRODUCTION | 11 |
| WHAT IS THE KINGDOM OF GOD? | 17 |
| **PART 2: MASTER BUILDER PRINCIPLES 1-3—AUTHORITY AND GREATNESS** | **25** |
| PRINCIPLE 1: RELEASING AUTHORITY IN THE KINGDOM | 27 |
| PRINCIPLE 2: KINGDOM GREATNESS—THE FIRST LESSON | 39 |
| THE SECOND LESSON ON KINGDOM GREATNESS | 49 |
| THE THIRD LESSON ON KINGDOM GREATNESS | 57 |
| PRINCIPLE 3: KINGDOM POWER | 63 |
| **PART 3: MASTER BUILDER PRINCIPLES 4-7—BECOMING AN OVERCOMER** | **73** |
| PRINCIPLE 4: OVERCOMING INSECURITY AND REJECTION | 75 |
| PRINCIPLE 5: DIVISION | 89 |
| PRINCIPLE 6: NEW WINE AND NEW WINE SKINS | 103 |
| PRINCIPLE 8: AMBITION—IS IT FROM HEAVEN OR EARTH? | 107 |
| **PART 4: MASTER BUILDER PRINCIPLES 8-9—HUMILITY AND THE CROSS** | **119** |
| PRINCIPLE 8: HUMILITY, PART 1 | 121 |
| HUMILITY, PART 2—PETER'S PATH TO LEADERSHIP | 131 |

| | |
|---|---|
| HUMILITY, PART 3—DWELLING WITH GOD | 139 |
| PRINCIPLE 9: THE CROSS—THE GREATEST MYSTERY OF THE KINGDOM | 149 |
| THE POWER OF THE CROSS—ANOTHER KEY OF THE KINGDOM | 159 |
| REVELATIONS OF THE WORK OF THE CROSS | 165 |
| **PART 5: KINGDOM MASTER BUILDERS OF THE BIBLE** | **169** |
| MOSES, THE MEEKEST OF ALL | 171 |
| THE APOSTLE PAUL: THE WORST SINNER & LEAST APOSTLE | 177 |
| KING DAVID, THE SWEET PSALMIST OF ISRAEL | 185 |
| THE APOSTLE PETER—LEADER OF LEADERS | 199 |

# FOREWORD

I met Scott in 2013. At the time, I lived near Austin, Texas, while Scott lived near New Haven, Connecticut. Our friendship began when Scott and a few other people were tasked with the job of finding a new lead pastor for Gateway Christian Fellowship in West Haven, Connecticut. While they were looking for a new leader, I was looking for a new assignment; and providence saw it fit for us to come together and have fun while laboring for the kingdom of God. Scott serves as one of our pastors, and is our board treasurer. More than that, since the autumn of 2013, Scott and I have become great friends. I have seen him overcome challenges, maintain a dedicated and passionate heart for Jesus, love his wife and children faithfully, and disciple others. If I've learned much about Scott in the last six years, it's this: he is fervent about others having an intimate relationship with Jesus, and he is a gifted communicator whose messages are born through prayer and study and tested through the fire of adversity.

I have discovered that real learning happens when the truth is applied. I've repeatedly seen Scott apply truth so lives are transformed—both his own and others. I believe that you will experience similar moments as you read *Kingdom Master Builders*. Scott's heart to help the body of Christ leave a lasting legacy is found when he tells us this book shows leaders how they can become wise master builders. Scott is a humble, wise, and loving leader who has a track record of building people. That's what lasts. Buildings may stand the test of time and defy the power of Mother Nature, but buildings do not transform hearts, heal broken lives, empower for service, stimulate big-dreaming, or do works of justice. People do that. In this book, you will find principles that serve as a blueprint for how to build lives that pass on kingdom values and truths from one generation to the next. It's the Holy Spirit working *through people* that transforms hearts, heal broken lives, empowers others for service, stimulates dreaming, and does works of justice. *It's people.* From talking about the principles of kingdom authority and greatness, to becoming an overcomer, to a much-needed humility found in the cross of Jesus Christ, Scott reveals how we are to engage the heart of God and become wise kingdom master builders.

The principles that Scott lays out in this helpful and timely book are expressions of the manifest presence of the Holy Spirit. Principles, precepts, signs, miracles, and wonders all point to a person—namely Jesus Christ. That's where the real power behind this collected work of truth comes from. As I read this book, my heart was ignited to know Christ more deeply and to understand how Christ wants to show up in the world through my life. It would be unfortunate if all you did was read this book to gather a few principles or apply a few concepts. The power of the principles that Scott eloquently writes about is found in a relationship with Jesus Christ. So as you read, pause to consider what you are reading, reflect upon it, and let it lead you in a conversation with God. While Scott writes to help us become wise kingdom master builders, it's the relationship with God found within these truths that will form us into the very people that Scott writes about.

So congratulations for having a copy of this book! I have a few suggestions for you. First, buy a copy for a friend and read it together. Learning and growing happen best in a group setting. Second, mark up the book—make notes and pray about what you learn. Third, share with your friends through conversation, texts, social media, or email how this book is adding value to your life. I'm excited about what your life will look for like Jesus because of this book. Receive the help, instruction, and encouragement that Scott is offering, so you and Christ can leave a lasting legacy as kingdom master builders.

Building together,

**—Lance Bane**
Lead Pastor, Gateway Christian Fellowship
www.lancebane.com

# PART 1: INTRODUCTION TO THE KINGDOM OF GOD

# INTRODUCTION

The title of this book, *Kingdom Master Builders*, comes out of a discussion Paul had with the Corinthian church. He told the Corinthian church that they are God's building and by the grace of God bestowed on him, he was a wise master builder, helping build God's building. He was a leader in the church. The people are the building in the body of Christ, the church; and that building is built in the kingdom of God. Just because you are a leader, it does not mean that you are a wise master builder. Good builders need to learn their trade, as do those who inspire to lead and become a master builder in the kingdom of God.

The purpose of this book is to show leaders how they can become wise master builders. Builders build; leaders influence people. The more effective leaders are, the more they can influence people. In a secular sense, we can say that leaders will intentionally guide people toward a certain culture, meaning the behaviors and beliefs characteristic of a particular social, ethnic, or age group. The culture we want to lead people to is the culture of the "kingdom of God." Kingdom builders who lead will influence people. They intentionally guide and direct people toward the behaviors, beliefs, and characteristics of God's kingdom, and they do that with kingdom principles. Operating with kingdom principles means that we have a lifestyle which allows the authority that rests in the kingdom to work through us. So it isn't just about that fact that we influence people for the kingdom, but it is how we do it. Those who become master builders will lead and guide with principles that govern and release power and authority of the kingdom in their lives and in the lives of those around them. Jesus demonstrated this in His life and ministry through relational connection with God the Father and the people around Him.

This is not a "how to" book on leadership, nor is it "steps to be an effective leader." It's about having God influence us, and then God influencing people *through* us. Whether we realize it or not, we all can lead. Someone who can influence anyone in anything is a leader. So here's the question: Is your leadership building the kingdom of God's influence in those around you?

When Jesus came to the earth, His message was about the kingdom. In the early chapters of the Gospels, He taught about the characteristics of the kingdom. He taught about the power and authority that we will have in the kingdom. As time went on, He taught the disciples how to operate in the kingdom. He wanted them to influence people around them for the kingdom; at the same time, He also wanted them to do it with kingdom integrity and principles which allow kingdom authority to work in and through them.

The message about the kingdom of God was something that people at that time had great interest in, because almost all lands were ruled by kings. The king generally had universal power and authority in their kingdom. Because of Old Testament prophesies, the Jewish people knew that Jehovah was going to send someone who was like Moses— but even greater—to be their ruler. They also understood that He would be from David's family line and He would establish a greater kingdom because this person would be the Messiah. They knew that God said He was going to establish a more glorious kingdom than David's or Solomon's.

The Jewish people were anxiously awaiting this Messiah because they lived in a kingdom ruled by the Romans, Gentiles who ignored Jewish customs and religious laws. The Jews were oppressed and controlled, so they eagerly awaited this king who they thought was going to free

## INTRODUCTION

them from the Romans, use His power and authority to defeat Rome, and establish an earthly authority like David's kingdom. They looked forward to ruling the world as God's people and being what God had promised—a special people, a royal priesthood, and a chosen people unto God.

So when Jesus started His ministry and began talking about the "kingdom," His message got people's attention. He told them to repent or change their ways because the "kingdom of God was at hand." Jesus went throughout the region proclaiming the gospel of the kingdom. During His ministry on earth, He explained how the kingdom worked, who would be great in the kingdom, who could inherit the kingdom, how to pray with kingdom authority, and how to act in kingdom authority. He also told them that He would give them the keys to the kingdom. He explained the mysteries of the kingdom. He told us to seek first this kingdom.

When Jesus rose from the dead, He spent forty days talking about things concerning the kingdom. In Acts 1:6-8, we read the last question that Jesus was asked before He ascended to heaven:

> So when they had come together, they were asking Him, saying, "Lord, is it at this time you are restoring the kingdom to Israel?" He said to them, "It is not for you to know times or epochs which the Father has fixed by His own authority; But you will receive power when the Holy Spirit has come upon you; and you shall be my witnesses both in Jerusalem, and in all Judea and Samaria, and even to the remotest part of the earth."

But when Jesus described who would enter the kingdom, who would be great in the kingdom, and how the kingdom would work, His answers were very different from what the Jewish people were expecting.

We can see that disconnect in the conversations Jesus had with the soon-to-be apostles. They came to know that Jesus was the Messiah and thought that because He was the Messiah, He was going to be the one who would set up His kingdom and get rid of the Roman control over them. They also thought that because they were the ones who Jesus called to be His leaders, that they would be given power and authority to run the kingdom. Therefore, they kept having the conversation with each other about who would be the greatest among them. They were all vying for the highest position of authority and power under Jesus. Jesus continually tried to get them to understand what God's kingdom was and was not. He was also trying to lead them to a place where they could walk in power and authority in God's kingdom and be able to avoid the same traps that men always fall into when they get too much power and authority.

Jesus knows that men crave power and authority. The desire for power is what led Lucifer to turn from God to himself, which led to his fall from heaven. The desire for power led Adam and Eve to turn from God and eat of the tree of the knowledge of good and evil. Through authority and power, men and angels have thought that they can control their own destinies and fulfill every want and desire. Authority and power have the potential to corrupt even the most even keeled and gentlest soul.

We often want to open our own doors, and the resulting fruit from those actions haven't quite been what God wanted—and maybe not what we intended either. Abraham waited for the promise of Isaac with nothing happening for years, when his wife figured out a way to help God give them an heir. They found a way on their own to get the promised child, and Abraham had a child with his servant, Hagar. That was not God's plan and the result turned out to be a problem that has extended even to this day—enmity between Israel and all the Arabic countries that are still trying to destroy her. We can know the plan of God, but we should be cautious about pursuing it with our wrong motives and deception. When we don't see things the way God sees and act the way God does, then we are deceived; another way to put it is our level of truthfulness and spiritual understanding is determined by the extent that we see things the way God does.

# INTRODUCTION

Jesus had a conversation with Peter and the disciples as recoded in Matthew 16 where he told them that He was going to give them the keys to the kingdom, meaning keys that would unlock the authority of God's kingdom in us and through us. With all this potential, have we really impacted the world as much as we should? Or is there more understanding we need for how to use the "keys of the kingdom"? I tend to think that although we have the keys, we need to learn how to use them more effectively in order to open the doors that the keys are supposed to give us access to. The following pages will reveal a key that opens the kingdom— and you can't open any other door in the kingdom until you learn about the characteristics of the key described in this book. You can consider it to be the key of all keys. Let's look at this key with some scriptures and stories from the New Testament.

Jesus impacted the world by His ministry in three-and-a-half years— in a way no man has ever done. How did He do that? I know He was the Son of God in the flesh, but He still was a man who was subject to the same human weakness, faults, and shortcoming that we all deal with. He did not succumb, but He overcame. How did He overcome? I believe these principles are revealed to us through His life and the lives of those He worked with. One thing that always stands out to me is that Jesus said that He only did what He saw the Father do (John 5). He was in complete unity with the Father and the Holy Spirit. He lived in a different kingdom, under different principles, and became the King of highest authority.

My desire is that this book will bring an understanding of how Jesus lived in that kingdom, how He released the authority and power of the kingdom in this world, and how that same authority and power can be released in and through us to lead others and impact the world around us. That is when we become Kingdom Master Builders.

# WHAT IS THE KINGDOM OF GOD?

As we discussed in the introduction, there have always been many misconceptions of what was and is the kingdom of God. Most of our misconceptions about this spiritual subject are the result of trying to understand spiritual principles using earthly and fleshly methods. For example, the only way the Jews generally thought about the kingdom was in terms of conquering the Romans and setting up a kingdom like David did—a physical kingdom, ruled by a king. They had no concept that God's kingdom is first and foremost a spiritual kingdom; otherwise the authority of the spiritual kingdom would affect the physical kingdom.

Let's look at how Jesus describes the kingdom of God. This subject was important to Jesus! From the very beginning of His ministry, Jesus constantly talked about the kingdom of God and the kingdom of heaven. We read in the beginning of the book of Mark that Jesus started His preaching by proclaiming, "**The time is fulfilled, and the kingdom of God is at hand; repent and believe in the gospel**" (Mark 1:1). In the beginning of Matthew chapter 3, John the Baptist was telling people to repent because "the kingdom of heaven is at hand." In chapter 4, we see that Jesus started to preach the same thing. In the book of Matthew there are 114 references to Jesus talking about the kingdom of heaven. Between all four Gospels, there are 188 references to the kingdom of God, most of which are in Mark and Luke. In Acts 1, we read that after Jesus rose from the dead and appeared to His disciples, He talked to them *for forty days* about things concerning the kingdom. So it shouldn't take a lot of spiritual perception to realize that the message of the kingdom was of central importance to what Jesus was expounding to the people. After being taught by Jesus about the kingdom in his early ministry, and even after He rose from the dead, the disciples still did not understand that the kingdom was first and foremost a spiritual kingdom. They continued to Jesus whether He was going to restore the kingdom to Israel, still thinking that He was going to set up His earthly kingdom, just like any other king would.

Jesus began to shed insight on this in the gospel of Luke:

> Now having been questioned by the Pharisees as to when the kingdom of God was coming, He answered them and said, "The kingdom of God is not coming with signs to be observed; Nor will they say, 'Look, here it is!' or, 'There it is!' For behold, the kingdom of God is in your midst (within you)" (Luke 17:20-21).

The word *kingdom* refers to dominion and encompasses the influence of the dominion or will of God within the hearts and minds of men. We get insight into this in the Lord's Prayer, when Jesus prayed for His kingdom to come and His will to be done, on earth as it is in heaven. In heaven, the kingdom of God exists because His perfect will is affecting the hearts of all creatures there, and as a result, His dominion rules all of heaven. It is a dominion that enables each person to be willing to follow Him of their own free will because of the perfection, beauty and holiness of the King. Holiness is a result of the attributes and character of God that transcend all measurement. God's wisdom, love, kindness, mercy, and power transcend any measurement or comparison to anyone else who possesses those qualities. To put this another way, if there were any charts on this, God would be "off the charts" in everything. This is what captivates us about God, and then causes us to willingly submit to Him. It is not forced or manipulated; it doesn't happen because of fear of retribution if we don't submit to Him—it is motivated by the love of God and the perfection of His holiness and righteousness.

# WHAT IS THE KINGDOM OF GOD?

Because the earth was under the power of the evil one during the time when Jesus walked the earth, God's will in the lives of men was very limited. When the devil was tempting Jesus in the wilderness (Luke 4:6-8), he tried to get Jesus to bow down and worship him, promising to give Him dominion over all the kingdoms the devil ruled, The devil had rulership over the whole world and had power over all kingdoms.

So the question is: Who gave this dominion and power to Satan? Well, the answer goes back to the book of Genesis. In the first chapter, we read that when God created man, He gave him dominion over this earth and all that was in it. God created man as His own offspring. As a child comes forth from a mother's womb, so man came forth from God. God formed his body out of the dust of the ground. Imagine the creativity of the master, to form such intricate beings such as us! But although He created this wonderful body, it would not be alive until He breathed in us the breath of life—the Spirit of life. God is Spirit, so He took some of His own nature, His essence of being—His glory—and put it in us. God choose to take from Himself and make us, which is essentially what happens when a child comes forth from the union of a man and woman. Man had the life of God in him. He communed with God and had an intimate fellowship with God. As we read in Psalm 8, the Psalmist is meditating on how God made us a little lower than Himself and crowned us with glory and honor. Man was made in the image and likeness of God and crowned with a crown of glory. We had a special position before the Father; we were His offspring, His family with whom He shared His kingdom and had intimate fellowship. Some translations say that we are made a little lower than angels, but that is not the correct translation. The Hebrew word used here is "Elohim," which is translated as "God" everywhere else. *We are made a little lower than God.*

This sets up an interesting situation and insight on why Lucifer (the devil) wanted to deceive man and separate himself from a Holy God. As described by prophet Isaiah, (Isaiah 14), Lucifer was the "Anointed Cherub" who covers. He was the highest of angels who covered the throne, so God's glory and beauty shown through him and he was the most highly exalted of all created beings. But because pride and inequity were found in him, he tried to exalt himself above God. He was stripped of his place and position and was cast out of heaven.

Then Lucifer watched God create a being (man) who was higher than he was, one who has God's breath, was of God's likeness, and was God's offspring. God crowned man with glory and honor and exalted him to the highest place of honor and authority in His kingdom. He put man on earth and told him to rule and reign over everything on earth. Man was to guide, guard, and govern this world. So jealousy was burning in Lucifer's heart and he began devising how to take this away from man. He came up with a plan that would lead them down the same path he traveled—a path which involved questioning God and exalting himself more than God.

God told Adam and Eve that they could eat from any tree in the garden, even the Tree of Life, but they could not eat from the Tree of Knowledge of Good and Evil. If they ate from that tree, that they would surely die, or a better translation would say, "in dying they will die." So when Adam and Eve listened to the deception and lies of the evil one and ate of the tree, they received the knowledge of both good and evil. They died spiritually, separated themselves from the life of God, and came under the influence of fleshly desires more than spiritual desires, which could be manipulated by the devil.

The dynamic force of life and the influence of the life of God was gone. So now the dominion and the will of God was very much hidden from man. It was easier and more comfortable for him to be influenced by evil and the evil one. Dominion was lost as well as the influence of the kingdom.

When God confronted Adam and Eve and showed them their error and the results thereof, He immediately made a plan for His influence in the heart and life of man to be reinstated again. It started in Genesis, advanced in the old covenant, and was sealed with the new covenant and Jesus' death, burial, and resurrection. It will reach its goal when the events of the book of Revelation finally unfold.

## WHAT IS THE KINGDOM OF GOD?

The kingdom of God could only influence man from "the fall" in Genesis to the fulfilling of the old covenant in the Gospels, which were consummated with Jesus' death on the cross and subsequent resurrection. You will notice in the Gospels that the preaching was about the kingdom being "at hand," which meant that the kingdom was coming and was near. Whenever the kingdom of God comes near, the power of God's dominion is present. When He started His ministry, Jesus proclaimed the kingdom, and then He would heal the sick, cleanse the leper, and cast out demons. These works were all effects of the kingdom of God coming near. The dominion and the power of God was present, so it uprooted the effects of the evil dominion and exerted its power against them.

**Jesus** also said something very interesting in the Gospels which always perplexed me until I started to understand that the kingdom, or dominion, of God was not in man until the New Testament was set into motion. He said in Luke 7:28, "I say to you, among those born of women there is no one greater than John; yet he who is least in the kingdom of God is greater than he." Jesus commended His first cousin in the flesh, John, by saying that he was as great as any man in the Old Testament; he was as great as Abraham, Isaac, Jacob, Moses, David, and Solomon. That was quite a pedestal He put John on—but then He proceeded to say that "the least" who made it into the kingdom was greater than John the Baptist. Why? Because all those great Old Testament men were still spiritually dead and separated from God. They knew who God was, they could experience the blessings of the old covenant and the relationship with God based on the works of the law. The Spirit of God could come upon them as He did mostly with the kings, prophets, and the high priests. But the Spirit of God could not dwell in man at that point, because man was spiritually dead.

The work of Jesus on earth and then His sacrifice on the cross brought new birth to man, which provided a way for the remission of sins. Once sin was taken away and the price was paid for the penalty of sin, Jesus provided a path where our spirit could be recreated in the image and likeness of Him once again. We could be spiritually born again, translated out of the kingdom of darkness into the kingdom of God. I love the way Paul writes in 2 Corinthians 4:6 and I paraphrase), The God, who said, "let there be light (or "light be," which was referring to Genesis chapter 1 of the creation) has shown in our hearts to give us the light of the knowledge of the glory of God in the face of Christ. Our sin caused us to fall short of His glory and made it impossible for us to live in His glory, no matter how hard we tried. So God created a path where His glory came down from heaven and took us back up there with Him. Therefore, the moment we say yes to Jesus and receive His work and forgiveness, God speaks to our spirit and says, "Light be." Forgiveness and redemption is received, and our spirit is recreated and seen in the same way as Jesus. We are put into the kingdom as a citizen and can live with all the privileges of the kingdom. Therefore, the least in the kingdom is greater than the highest of prophets of the old covenant.

I like the way Paul describes what happens at new birth. He does it in so many ways!

> Giving thanks unto the Father, which hath made us meet to be partakers of the inheritance of the saints in light: who hath **delivered us from the power of darkness, and hath translated us into the kingdom of his dear Son** (Colossians 1:12-13 KJV).

We have been delivered from the power—or better translated, the *authority* of darkness—of the kingdom of darkness, and translated into the kingdom of His dear Son, which is the kingdom of God. The word *translated* here means to be moved from one place to another. So when we say yes to God and to the work of Jesus, He recreates our spirit in the image and likeness of God. Then the glory of God is breathed back into us, we become spiritually alive, we are *moved into* the kingdom of God, and then we are made citizens of that kingdom!

Now that we are in the kingdom, Jesus told us to seek first the kingdom of God and His righteousness (Matthew 6:33). If the kingdom is within us, then we need to learn how to allow this kingdom to have authority and influence over our actions, thinking, and entire being. It is through the Lord's Prayer: "Your kingdom come, your will be done on earth as it is in heaven." Because the kingdom is inside us, Jesus was praying for the will of the kingdom be done on earth. Although we can think more "macro" about this and believe that this refers to the whole planet, I would rather take a "micro" look at this, because our bodies are made from this earth. God formed us from the dust of the ground and then breathed in us the (breath) spirit of life—His very presence. The earth is each of us; we should pray that His will be done on earth (in us) as it is in heaven.

Once the kingdom comes to each person, and each person agrees with the will of God, then the kingdom grows and inhabits the whole earth. Let us pray that prayer as we read the words in this book and by the grace of God, the revelation that is found in these pages will help move each of us down that path.

# PART 2: MASTER BUILDER PRINCIPLES 1-3—AUTHORITY AND GREATNESS

# PRINCIPLE 1: RELEASING AUTHORITY IN THE KINGDOM

One evening while I was in a prayer meeting with the pastors of my local fellowship, I wasn't feeling overly spiritual. I had worked a long day and was tired. To tell you the truth, I felt dry and I really didn't want to be there. As we began to pray, the atmosphere in the room began to change and the Spirit of the Lord rested on me. This happens to me periodically in my relationship with God, and when it does, it is clear that the Lord is speaking to me. That day I heard the Lord say, **"My leaders in the church desire power and authority to impact the world they live in, but they are not going to receive the authority of the Lion until they learn how to walk in the meekness of the Lamb." That's when I realized that in God's kingdom, the authority of the Lion is released in the meekness of the Lamb.**

When I heard these words, it felt like everything else was silent around me as I contemplated what the Lord had said. Being a leader in the local church for many years, I knew that I wanted authority to change the world around me; authority to help change my family. I wanted to see people's lives changed by the Lord Jesus Christ—I wanted them to be healed, delivered, and set free from the bondages and hurt that binds their souls. I wanted people to live in the peace and harmony that God has provided, and I wanted the world to understand that the principle of God living inside us will result in a more fulfilled and peaceful life in this world.

I have heard many people pray for power and authority to impact the world around them. Many of those prayers were earnest, heartfelt prayers, and from where I sit, they were uttered with the best intentions. As I am writing this, I recall the prayer the disciples prayed in Acts 4 after Peter and John were arrested and later released. Once they let everyone know what had happened, they prayed in one accord as we read in Acts 4:27-31:

> For truly in this city there were gathered together against Your holy servant Jesus, whom You anointed, both Herod and Pontius Pilate, along with the Gentiles and the peoples of Israel, to do whatever Your hand and Your purpose predestined to occur. And now, Lord, take note of their threats, **and grant that your bond-servants may speak your word with all confidence, while you extend your hand to heal, and signs and wonders take place through the name of your holy servant Jesus**." And when they had prayed, the place where **they had gathered together was shaken, and they were all filled with the Holy Spirit and began to speak the word of God with boldness.**

We know that the Lord answered their prayer, because we see in Acts 4:33 that "with great power the apostles were giving testimony to the resurrection of the Lord Jesus, and abundant grace was upon them all."

As I continued to contemplate the word about the lion and lamb, I thought about how the lion is the king of the jungle and the most feared of predators. As the king of the jungle, his roar would get the attention of everyone and everything around him. Jesus was prophetically called the Lion of the Tribe of Judah. Judah was ordained by God to be the ruling tribe in Israel. Jesus was going to be the top ruler. Jesus was also referred to as the Lamb of God. These two animals are totally opposite in their characteristics and authority. Lambs are weak, fearful, and unintimidating to any animal around. How could the characteristics of both work together to bring power and authority?

## PRINCIPLE 1: RELEASING AUTHORITY IN THE KINGDOM

As I was pondering these words, the Holy Spirit brought my attention to Revelation chapter five, which begins with John in heaven noticing a book with seven seals in the right hand of God. Then a strong angel steps up and asks a question, "Who is worthy to open the book and to break its seals?" John concludes that there wasn't anyone worthy to open the seals. He began to cry because there was no one in heaven or on earth or under the earth who was worthy to open the seals. Nobody seemed to answer the question, so John assumed that no one was worthy. But I think everyone in heaven knew the answer; they were observant to what was going on and were awed by the one worthy Person. They were captivated by who He was in all His magnificent beauty, power, and glory.

As I think about this, years later, it reminds me of how we are with God. Rather than wait, mediate, and observe what the Spirit of God is doing and saying, we immediately go into "baby mode" and start crying because we didn't think God answered us or because God didn't do what we thought He should do. If we would just be quiet and learn to observe the Holy Spirit and contemplate His ways, the answer is usually right in front of us—if we would just open our spiritual eyes and ears!

Now back to Revelation chapter five. Finally, one of the elders in heaven came graciously over to John and told him to stop crying. He explained that there is one worthy to open the seals: "the Lion of the Tribe of Judah, the Root of David—He is Worthy." I am sure John was relieved by these words. Then he looked over to the throne, as it is stated in Revelation 5:6-7:

> And I saw between the throne (with the four living creatures) and the elders **a Lamb standing, as if slain, having seven horns and seven eyes, which are the seven Spirits of God, sent out into all the earth**. And He came and took the book out of the right hand of Him who sat on the throne.

I am sure John was waiting to see a magnificent king, clothed with all the adornment of a king; one who had the majesty and strength of a lion. But he did not. Instead John saw "**a Lamb**," a meek, unintimidating lamb; one who had been slain. I am not sure what that would have looked like, but it was apparent that the lamb had massive injuries; it should have been dead but was alive. The marks of His "death" must have been very pronounced for John to describe it the way he did.

Another John—John the Baptist—introduced Jesus as "The Lamb of God," the messenger who was paving the way for the coming Messiah. He was in the wilderness proclaiming repentance, saying there was one coming who was greater than he. John was creating a great stir—so much that even the religious leaders of that day left the city and went out into the wilderness to hear him. John said of himself in Matthew 3:11:

> As for me, I baptize you with water for repentance, but He who is coming after me is mightier than I, and I am not fit to remove His sandals; He will baptize you with the Holy Spirit and fire.

John was saying something wonderful about the one coming, that he was not worthy to remove His sandals and that He was going to baptize them with Holy Spirit and Fire. When people heard this, they must have thought a mighty king was coming, one full of majesty and glory. Then when John baptized Jesus, he introduced Him as the "Lamb of God who takes away the sin of the world."

> The next day he saw Jesus coming to him and said, "Behold, the Lamb of God who takes away the sin of the world! This is He on behalf of whom I said, 'after me comes a Man who has a higher rank than I, for He existed before me.' I did not recognize Him, but so that He might be manifested to Israel, I came baptizing in water." John testified saying, "I have seen the Spirit descending as a dove out of heaven, and He remained upon Him. I did not recognize Him, but He who sent me to baptize in water

## PRINCIPLE 1: RELEASING AUTHORITY IN THE KINGDOM

said to me, 'He upon whom you see the Spirit descending and remaining upon Him, this is the One who baptizes in the Holy Spirit.' I myself have seen and have testified that this is the Son of God" (John 1:29-34).

John the Baptist called Jesus the Lamb of God. He said that he did not recognize Him until he saw the heavens open and the Spirit descend on Him like a dove. Because Jesus was John's first cousin in the flesh, I am sure they had already met and grew up together. So he must have seen Jesus before. However, on that day when Jesus came to be baptized, God opened John's eyes and he not only called Jesus the "Lamb of God," but also "The Son of God." This had to be perplexing to the people who heard it: one who is a lamb, who is meek and is used as a sacrifice, and who is also the Son of God.

Look back at John the apostle's vision and you see the same conflict of descriptions. The Lion of the Tribe of Judah" and "The Root of David" are both terms which are prophetic descriptions for the coming Messiah, the king who was going to lead Israel and set up a kingdom greater than the kingdoms that David or Solomon established. Then we see this lion described as a "lamb that has been slain," but this lamb has seven horns and seven eyes. The seven horns represent power and honor as described in other visions and places in the Bible. The seven eyes represent the omniscience of God. There we have it: the image of the perfect unity of meekness, humility, and power in the ultimate ruler.

Before we go deeper into this scene, I would like to briefly give you some definitions, so you get more significance out of this scene. Years ago, while I was meditating on meekness, the Lord spoke to me and said, "Meekness is power under control, submitted to the will of God." Humility is meekness's close brother, it can be defined in several ways. Humility brings you to a place of complete dependence on God, a place of complete submission to God, a place where you completely accept the truth, where you understand that God is right and righteous, and that pride (the opposite of humility) is the explanation for every human error and weakness.

Go back to the scene in Revelation and notice the progression of statements made. First from the four living creatures and the twenty-four elders, then in the second chorus we add the angels and the myriads of thousands around the throne. Lastly, we add every created thing in heaven, earth, and under the earth.

In the first chorus, the four living creatures and the elders said, "Worthy is the Lamb to break the seals, for He was slain and purchased, and redeemed man." As described in Leviticus 16, Jesus was both the sacrificial lamb and the scapegoat offered on the Day of Atonement. Jesus not only brought forgiveness of sins, but as the scapegoat, He took the sins on Himself. He didn't just cover our sins, He took them and the penalty that came with them. He didn't just purchase us to pay for our sins and keep us from hell; He purchased us to make us a part of His kingdom—God's kingdom—and priests in that kingdom who have access to the King and the authority to reign with Him on this earth.

What is it about Jesus that makes Him worthy to break the seals? Was it the offering He made or the nature and character of His love and compassion that was demonstrated in that offering? The seals seem to release great havoc on the earth; judgment as some may think. I think Jesus was worthy because He is completely good and righteous—the only one pure enough in heart to release those judgments. God's heart is not about judgment, but sin will cause and demand judgment, and it will have to be done to restore the purity of the earth and His kingdom.

Then with one voice, many angels around the throne, the living creatures, and the elders all shout together, "Worthy is the Lamb that was slain, to receive power, riches, wisdom, might, glory, and blessing." All the terms used are of great power and authority that men strive for, and all the things that allow one to rule with the highest level of dominion and influence over the lives of people. But we need to understand that they did not say **"worthy is the Lion of the Tribe of Judah"** or **"worthy is the Root of David."** They said worthy is the meek, humble **"lamb who sacrificed Himself to redeem man."** It was the meekness and humility of the lamb which resulted in giving Him the authority of the lion, to

## PRINCIPLE 1: RELEASING AUTHORITY IN THE KINGDOM

become the King of Kings and receive the name at which every knee will bow and confess His lordship.

Then scripture records that every created thing in heaven, earth, under the earth, and in the sea cried out, "To Him who sits on the throne, and to the Lamb, be blessing, honor, and glory and dominion forever and ever." Scripture says that all dominion was given to the One who sits on the throne, who is the Father. They did not say to "the Son," but to "the Lamb." The book of Revelation reveals the authority of "the Lamb of God." The book mentions the Lamb of God twenty-nine times, and almost every time it recognizes the great authority and place that the Lamb of God has in the kingdom of God. It is a revelation of the Lamb of God, who received the highest place of power and authority in all of history. Jesus—the Lamb of God—is the King of Kings and sits in the highest place of authority in God's kingdom

This scene in heaven plays out what is spoken by the Apostle Paul in Philippians 2. This chapter can be referred to as the "emptying passage":

> Have this attitude in yourselves which was also in Christ Jesus, who, although He existed in the form of God, did not regard equality with God a thing to be grasped, but emptied Himself, taking the form of a bond-servant, and being made in the likeness of men. Being found in appearance as a man, He humbled Himself by becoming obedient to the point of death, even death on a cross. For this reason also, God highly exalted Him, and bestowed on Him the name which is above every name, so that at the name of Jesus every knee will bow, of those who are in heaven and on earth and under the earth, and that every tongue will confess that Jesus Christ is Lord, to the glory of God the Father (Philippians 2:5-11).

Let's consider what Jesus did and how He conquered. First, the Philippians passage says that Jesus' equality with God was not a thing to be grasped. I would rather say that Jesus' equality with God was not a thing He prized the most. He did not want to hold on to that power and position more than anything else. So the question bears asking: If Jesus didn't think being equal with God and sitting on the throne the most important thing, *then what was the most important thing?*

The most important thing to Jesus was pleasing the Father and doing His will; and the Father counted "MANKIND" as the prize! He wanted to redeem His offspring and bring them back to a place of union and fellowship with Him. Jesus emptied Himself of His heavenly glory, position, and power, came down in the flesh, shed His glory, and took on the same form and shape as His creation. He became a servant of God in a fleshly body.

Jesus had another great test as a man, because man tried to exalt Him as the conquering king and wanted to make Him a king over an earthly kingdom. But Jesus knew His kingship wouldn't come the same way the world places a king and a leader into position. Therefore, He rejected all the glory that man wanted to give Him, humbled Himself unto death, and allowed the "creation" to take the creator to death on the cross.

In Jesus' Sermon on the Mount, He said, "the meek will inherit the earth." Jesus showed the ultimate in meekness at the cross. Throughout His earthly ministry, every time the authorities tried to arrest Him, He would walk right through the crowd and foil their attempts to catch Him. This was because it wasn't time for them to take Him. But in the garden of Gethsemane, they came, and He let them take Him. One of the most interesting accounts of this was in John's gospel (John18:5-6), where Jesus asked, "Who have you come for?" and they replied, "Jesus of Nazareth." Most translations say that Jesus replied, "I am He" but, literally, He said "I AM," meaning He was the great I AM, the self-existing almighty God. They knew what Jesus was saying; they knew the Old Testament words of God when Moses asked, "Who shall I say that sends me to the children of Israel?" and He said, "I am that I am." Jesus had already said that He was the "I AM." In John 8, He said to the religious leaders of the day, "Before Abraham was, I AM." He also gave a greater description of the character of the "I am" when He said in

## PRINCIPLE 1: RELEASING AUTHORITY IN THE KINGDOM

John, "I AM the bread of life" (John 6:35; 41; 48; 51), "I AM the light of the world" (John 8:12; 9:5), "I AM the door to the sheepfold" (John 10:7), "I AM the good shepherd" (John 10:14), "I AM the resurrection and the life" (John 11:25), and lastly "I AM the way, the truth, and the life" (John 14:16).

John records that there was so much power in His words, that when He replied to the guards: "I AM," they fell back and hit the ground. The guards must have been awestruck, but even through their human frailty, the "Great I AM" allowed Himself to be taken. What a demonstration of meekness, goodness, and humility!

A similar situation happened when Jesus was before Pilot, (John 18:34-37; John 19:10-12). Pilot was questioning Jesus about what He had done. Jesus said His kingdom was not of this world, and if it were, His servants would be fighting for Him and He would not be handed over to the Jews. Pilot later found out that Jesus was being hailed as the Son of God. He was afraid and asked Jesus more questions because Pilot wanted to release Him, but Jesus would not answer Him.

> So Pilate said to Him, "You do not speak to me? Do you not know that I have authority to release you, and I have authority to crucify you?" Jesus answered, "You would have no authority over me, unless it had been given you from above; for this reason he who delivered me to you has the greater sin" (John 19:10-11).

Jesus knew His authority—He had the power to change the situation, but the will of the Father was that He would go to the cross and redeem man. What a demonstration of meekness! "It was power under control; submitted to the will of God.

This is how Jesus, the Lamb of God conquered: He has the authority of the Lion, but the authority and kingdom power are released through the meekness and humility of the Lamb. This is how Jesus operated the first time He came to earth, and it will be how He operates the second time He comes, because it is His character and nature. This type of authority and power cannot be understood in worldly ways; it confuses the devil and the worldly system. Listen to what Paul says about how this heavenly kingdom operates:

> Yet we do speak wisdom among those who are mature; a wisdom, however, not of this age nor of the rulers of this age, who are passing away; but we speak God's wisdom in a mystery, the hidden wisdom which God predestined before the age*s to our glory;* the wisdom which none of the rulers of this age has understood; for if they had understood it they would not have crucified the Lord of glory (1 Corinthians 2:6-8).

The kingdom of God operates on different principles than ours. When the earthly authorities took Jesus, they thought they had Him. From Adam to Jesus, the devil knew that he had authority on earth and that every man who died previously went to the lower parts of the earth. But this was the plan of God! The cross of Christ was the greatest "Trojan Horse" ever devised, because after Jesus died, He descended to the lower parts of the earth (Ephesians 4). Envision this: there's Jesus in the lower parts of the earth, and the devil and the workers of darkness thinking that they have defeated the Son of God. Suddenly, in the lower parts of earth with all the evil forces celebrating, the Holy Spirit of God shows up and breathes life back into Jesus, as we read in Romans 6. He was raised by the glory of the Father. Jesus being raised from death to life had to be one of the devil's worst nightmares! Jesus stripped the devil of his authority in the very pit of hell, taking the keys of death and life and providing us with the keys of the kingdom of God.

> When I saw Him, I fell at His feet like a dead man. And He placed His right hand on me, saying, "Do not be afraid; I am the first and the last, and the living One; and I was dead, and behold, **I am alive forevermore, and I have the keys of death and of Hades** (Revelation 1:17-18).

## PRINCIPLE 1: RELEASING AUTHORITY IN THE KINGDOM

In Matthew 27, the scripture states that after Jesus died, the graves of the saints who had died were opened, and the saints of old who had been in the lower parts of the earth (the place Jesus called "Abraham's bosom") were raised and were seen in the streets of Jerusalem.

Jesus did something no man had ever done before: He didn't sin or yield to the devil. He offered Himself as the spotless lamb for the redemption of man. He conquered in the greatest of battles through humility and meekness. He humbled himself to death by going to the cross. In the end, God exalted Jesus back to a place of even higher authority in heaven, and, as it says in Philippians 2, every knee will bow, both in heaven and earth, and under the earth, acknowledging that Jesus is Lord. The meekness and humility of the Lamb released the authority of heaven and the kingdom of God in every man's heart.

For us to really walk in the kingdom authority that God intended for us and to use that authority only for good and for the forwarding of the will of God, we need the meekness and the humility of the Lamb in our lives. This is a process that is continually at work in our lives, a process we need to allow God to work in us. If we do this, the authority of the Lion will work in and through us to bring the will and authority of the kingdom in our lives and the world around us.

# PRINCIPLE 2: KINGDOM GREATNESS—THE FIRST LESSON

In the Gospels we find a recurring discussion among the twelve disciples and Jesus regarding who is and what is the greatest in the kingdom. Some of the discussions came from the disciples asking Jesus who is the greatest. Others came from heated conversations among the disciples as to who was the greatest, and some came from even more heated discussions due to the disciples maneuvering for positions of greatness in the kingdom.

As I read the Gospels, I have found at least three separate discussions on the subject, which happened at different times. Because the Gospels are really a short synopsis of what Jesus did during His three-and-a-half-year ministry, I would say that this was an important subject for the disciples to understand.

It is also important to understand that when the disciples had this discussion, their thought of greatness in the kingdom and how to obtain it was much different than what Jesus was trying to get across to them. To the disciples, greatness in the kingdom was about who had the highest rank and who had the greatest authority to rule over people. Remember, it was still in the minds of the disciples that the Messiah was coming back to set up an earthly kingdom like King David's. So their thoughts went to all the benefits and authority that came with such positions.

They had image of being (as with David's kingdom on this earth) an under-ruler with Jesus as He governed.

The disciples did not understand that their motives were being corrupted by their selfish ambition. One of the best illustrations of this is in Matthew 16, where Peter received his greatest commendation and then his greatest correction by Jesus. Jesus asked the disciples, "Who do the people say the Son of Man is "and then asked the disciples who *they* thought He was. Peter answered Jesus by saying, "The Christ, the Son of the living God." Jesus commended Peter for this and went on to tell him that He was going to give Peter the keys to the kingdom of heaven, which would give Peter authority to use the power of heaven to bind and loose on earth. All kings and those who had authority on earth, could bind and loose as they pleased, meaning that they could enforce their will on people within their realm of authority only.

If the thought of who would have great authority when Jesus set up His kingdom was already on the disciples' minds, it must have fed into Peter's thinking even more that he would have authority in Jesus' earthly kingdom. First, he got a commendation from Jesus, and then based on Jesus' words, he probably thought that he had the inside track to the highest place of authority in Jesus' kingdom. I can just see pride and self-assuredness start to well up in Peter, as it would with most of us.

Directly after this, Matthew records that Jesus started to tell the disciples that He must go to Jerusalem and be mistreated by the religious leaders and then be killed by them, but He also said that after three days He would rise from the dead. Something must have gone off in Peter's thinking; he must have thought, "This doesn't compute…how could this be? If Jesus dies, what will happen to the kingdom He is going to set up? What will happen to my position? What about those keys He gave me?" Still feeling pumped up from his commendation, Peter figured he had to straighten Jesus out, and started to let Jesus know that this cannot be!

> From that time forth began Jesus to shew unto his disciples, how that he must go unto Jerusalem, and

## PRINCIPLE 2: KINGDOM GREATNESS—THE FIRST LESSON

> suffer many things of the elders and chief priests and scribes, and be killed, and be raised again the third day. Then Peter took him, and began to rebuke him, saying, be it far from thee, Lord: this shall not be unto thee (Matthew 16:21-22 KJV).

On the surface it appears like Peter is looking out for Jesus, trying to protect Him and keep Him from such a bad fate. This may have been part of Peter's motives—but it was not his primary intention. Jesus immediately said to Peter, "Get behind me Satan, you are an offense to me." What He was saying to Peter was, "You are getting in the way of the plans of God, because you are thinking primarily about yourself, your own self-promotion and position, and not the will of God." Peter was thinking of his own self-interests first; he allowed selfishness to enter in. Selfishness will always lead to sin and evil. Selfishness led Adam and Eve to eat of the tree; they were looking to their own benefit, thinking they could help God by giving themselves more than they already had. Selfishness and selfish ambition are like a cloud over your spiritual eyes and ears that will not allow you to discern the ways of God or why His plan is always the best.

Jesus went on to tell Peter, "What does it profit a man to gain the whole world and lose his soul?" If you look at this from Peter's viewpoint, he thought Jesus had given him the highest place of authority and power in the earthly kingdom that Jesus was setting up. Rulers try to rule and gain as much power and authority to rule as they can. When rulers are obsessed with gaining power, people become pawns for the growth of their kingdoms.

When God first created man, the scriptures record that God formed man out of the dust of the ground and then breathed His Spirit into him. He took some of His own essence and nature and created man. As a woman gives birth to a child, so God gave birth to man. When man received the breath or spirit of life, he became a living soul. Living souls are souls infused with the life of God. Man's soul can lose the true nature and forces of life if he chooses evil, selfishness, and sin and separates himself from God. It's our choice; it was what Adam and Eve did, and this is the path that Peter was on.

Jesus said something that, in hindsight, we might understand, but at that moment it must have been a difficult statement for the disciples—He said, "Take up your cross and follow me." They didn't understand yet what Jesus was going to do. Later they understood that it was the will of God for Jesus to go to the cross to redeem man, and that it was Jesus' alone to bear. Each of us has a cross to bear; we need to put aside our selfish desires and ambitions and say to God, "Not my will, but Your will be done on earth (in us because our bodies are made of earth, the dust of the ground) as it is in heaven."

By outer appearance, Peter may have looked good, even spiritual by trying to protect Jesus. When the light of God's word came, it exposed the true thoughts and intentions of his heart. Similarly, when that happens in our lives, each of us will have the choice to change and acknowledge our motives or hold onto them and be exposed later before the judgment seat of Christ (2 Corinthians 5:10). Here is where we will be judged for our deeds done in the body, both good and evil.

Let's discuss each of the situations which address the disciples' arguments regarding who was the greatest in the kingdom of God. The first one is recorded in Matthew 18:1-6, Luke 9:46-48, and Mark 9:33-40. I am going to use Matthew's version, but would encourage you to mediate on each one these versions. Matthew recorded the following:

> At about the same time, the disciples came to Jesus asking, "Who gets the highest rank in God's kingdom?" For an answer Jesus called over a child, whom he stood in the middle of the room, and said, "I'm telling you, once and for all, that unless you return to square one and start over like children, you're not even going to get a look at the kingdom, let alone get in. Whoever becomes simple and elemental again, like this child, will rank high in God's kingdom. What's more, when you receive the

## PRINCIPLE 2: KINGDOM GREATNESS—THE FIRST LESSON

childlike on my account, it's the same as receiving me" (Matthew 18:1-5 MSG).

I love the way *The Message* translation interprets this scripture. I believe it amplifies the original intent, which was to say to the disciples, "Don't you understand? If you guys want to be great and have great authority as leaders in the kingdom, first you must at least get *into* the kingdom! And if you don't get in, how are you going to be leaders with great authority to rule and lead? If you don't become like a little child, you will not get in at all!"

So what are the characteristics of a "little child" that Jesus was talking about? First, a little child is almost completely dependent on his or her parents. A little child in the kingdom must come to a place of complete dependence on God—that is a good definition of humility. Humility is a spiritual state where God is all, and you are nothing. Humility is a place where you put no confidence in your earthly ability and power, your organizational skills, your leadership skills, your intimidation skills, or any other earthly, carnal skill though which you can gain success. I like what Paul said to the Corinthians. He told them that he did not come to them with the greatest of speech or oratory skills or as a highly educated man, but instead with much weakness, fear, and trembling. His speech was in demonstration of the Spirit and power, so their faith would not be in Him or on Him, but on God.

Second, little children are not concerned with position and what they can get from you. They are open, they love unconditionally, there is no malice in their heart, they don't have selfish ambition, they are able to be guided, and they like to believe the best about people. They tend to be pure in heart and motives and uncorrupted by the world and the things that the world inflicts on us. Just think how enjoyable it is to watch a young child who is pure in heart, simply unaware of his or her surroundings, just loving to play and enjoy the people around.

Based on the times and customs of the day in which Jesus lived, age was regarded and respected very highly. One's position in the society was often dictated based on age. This is also illustrated in Jesus' discussion on the subject in Luke 22:26, "But it is not this way with you, but the one who is the greatest among you **must become like the youngest**, and the leader like the servant." The youngest was the greatest. Jesus also said something even more radical: Governors and leaders are not the greatest, but the ones who serve the governors and leaders were greater. Jesus was shaking things up again, taking common religious and social thought of the time and turning it upside down.

This was the opposite of the disciples' tendencies. They had selfish ambition and wanted to be the ones who were served because of their position of authority, always jockeying for position either directly or indirectly before Jesus. They were using their position to create a special group, and if you weren't part of their group, you couldn't use the things Jesus taught. This was demonstrated when they tried to stop someone who wasn't part of their group from casting out a demon. Jesus told them not to do that because other people besides those in their group can also use the things He taught and do the works of God.

The disciples demonstrated that they could be tempted to use their authority to hurt other people when they wanted to call fire down from heaven after the Samaritans told Jesus not to come through the country if He was not going to stop there. Jesus told them that they didn't know what kind of spirit they were of. Also, there was a situation previously talked about regarding Peter's selfish ambition, which so blinded him that he could not see the plans of God and tried to stop Jesus from going to the cross.

But before we keep hammering the disciples on all these issues, we need to realize that all the same weakness and frailties can be found in all of us. If we don't learn to be like that little child Jesus talked about, then the same weaknesses the disciples had will manifest in our lives too.

As I was reading Peter's epistles, I realized that Peter did grasp these truths and had them worked into his spiritual life. Look at what he wrote in 1 Peter 2:1-3:

## PRINCIPLE 2: KINGDOM GREATNESS—THE FIRST LESSON

> Therefore, **putting aside all malice and all deceit and hypocrisy and envy and all slander**, like newborn babies, long for the pure milk of the word, so that by it you may grow up in your salvation, if you have tasted the kindness of the Lord.

For years I have taught this scripture and would always concentrate on the part that said, "Long for the pure milk of the word." One day I read this and realized that Peter understood what Jesus was talking about in the Gospels—and he even took it a step further. First, he realized that man can easily have malice in his heart, which is a preconceived plan to place your own desires over the desires of God and others, which is fueled by deceit and layered with all types of hypocrisy. This primarily comes from envy, whether it is of earthly or spiritual things. Peter did not say, "Be like a little child;" he said, "Go back further and become like a newborn baby who has no ability to take care of himself, and just desire the pure nourishment of God and His Word, so you may grow into the person God wants you to be—one who can become great in the kingdom and great as a leader, because you're a servant-leader who always looks for the wellbeing of others and the will of God first before any self-promotion."

Malice and envy will cause you to rejoice in watching others fail if it furthers your own promotion. It will also push us to expose peoples' weaknesses and faults, rather than protect others and help them through their issues and errors. These two "evil cousins" will cause division and deception. We often don't even realize that we are operating with these motives until things in life expose them. Peter was probably not aware of how subject he was to these things until Jesus exposed his selfish ambition.

Please remember that no matter how successful we may be in life or ministry; these things can invade us in ways we don't realize. Let's ask ourselves a few questions: Do we always have to prove ourselves right? Do we sacrifice or hurt other people to maintain our positions of authority? Will we agree with people in authority, even though in our hearts we believe they are wrong, because disagreement will lead to falling out of favor and loss of our position?

I would challenge you to bring these questions before the Lord, sit in His presence, ask Him if any of these are true in you, and see what happens.

James wrote about these things and said that when there is jealousy and selfish ambition in our hearts, there is disorder and every evil thing (see James 3:16). But God's wisdom is generated out of meekness. God's wisdom is pure in its motives. It is meek and full of mercy, which leads to forgiveness. It will bring peace to you and others.

There are numerous times in the Gospels when Peter is used as an example of what you shouldn't do. What I notice in the Bible is the transformation of Peter from a rash, impulsive person who wanted to be the greatest of the apostles, to a humble person who learned these principles about how to walk in the kingdom. I see the process manifesting itself as Peter denied Christ. He was distraught, an utter failure, a boaster who vowed that he would never to leave Jesus, claiming that he would instead protect Him. But he ended up doing the very thing Jesus prophesied—denying Him three times.

I can feel the depth of despair Peter must have had after the third denial. In Luke 22:61, we read that when the rooster crowed, the Lord looked at Peter and their eyes caught. Like a flood, Peter was overwhelmed by despair, realizing he denied the Lord, just as He said he would.

Jesus died on the cross. It is recorded that only John was there with Jesus' natural birth mother. Peter was probably off somewhere in despair and depression. He must have been thinking of the great things Jesus did—the things *they* did together, the visions he had of serving with Jesus as a man with authority in His kingdom. All of it instantly dissolved in a moment's time.

## PRINCIPLE 2: KINGDOM GREATNESS—THE FIRST LESSON

Then Peter hears from the women that Jesus rose from the dead. Peter ran to the tomb to see what had happened; finding only Jesus' grave clothes. Jesus appeared to some of the disciples and the apostles a few times and He talked to them about what had happened. Peter, although listening intently, must have been thinking, "I denied the Lord after making such a vow to protect and stay with him."

Then finally Jesus appeared to the disciples a third time while they were fishing. This time, Jesus started talking to Peter and asked him a question that was like a dagger straight to his wounded heart. In John 21:15, we read that Jesus asks Peter, "Peter, do you love me more than any of the other disciples?" The word Jesus used was *agape* which is a Greek word meaning "unconditional love." Jesus asked the question because Peter had previously said that even if the others left, he would not boasting that he loved Jesus more than the others and was more committed to Him than anyone else.

Peter must have thought, "What can I say now? I have shown Him that I did not love Him as much." But he answered truthfully, "I love you" (which in this case is *phileo*, a Greek word meaning "to have deep brotherly affection for"), although Peter didn't actually say it, it was implied by the word he used. After this, Jesus told Peter to go "feed His sheep." Peter was shocked at this statement. He probably thought his failure disqualified him from ever being a great leader in God's kingdom. Then Jesus asked Peter the same question two more times. He probably asked him a total of three times because Peter had denied him three times. Jesus may have also asked three times because Peter was the one who asked Jesus in Matthew 18:21, "How many times should we forgive a brother who sinned against us? Seven times (Paraphrase)?" Jesus' response was, "Seventy times seven." I find it interesting that after that conversation Jesus told a parable about the kingdom of heaven and forgiveness. Peter sinned three times and Jesus forgave him three times.

Jesus said, "Peter I forgive you and love you unconditionally. I have called you to feed My sheep." Peter learned that Jesus' commitment to him was much more than his could ever be. This process brought a submission and humility in Peter's life that led him to be one of "the greatest." Let's continue down that path so we can learn and receive the same transforming power that Peter received.

# THE SECOND LESSON ON KINGDOM GREATNESS

Let's venture into another conversation Jesus had with His disciples about who was the greatest and how authority would work in the kingdom. If we fast-forward to the latter part of Jesus' ministry on earth, we find that the disciples were still vying for position—even after being with Him for three years—and were still having arguments about who was the greatest, either in their minds or out loud with each other. There was an instance when the mother of James and John asked Jesus if her sons could sit on Jesus' right and left hand in His kingdom. This request came right after Jesus explained that He was going to Jerusalem and would be mistreated and beaten by the religious leaders of the time, condemned to death, and on the third day rise again.

It was obvious that the disciples had very little understanding of what was really going to happen to Jesus. Here was a man who had casted out demons, raised the dead-on numerous occasions, restored withered hands, healed people who were paralyzed, and spoke to the weather and it obeyed Him. On top of all this, John said in his gospel that there were so many other things that Jesus did, that they were too numerous to be recorded. To be fair to the disciples, we would be no different than they were in the current circumstances. How could someone with such power and authority be taken and killed by religious leaders who had not been able to touch Him for three years?

The only way that happened is because Jesus allowed them to take Him. The disciples must have asked Him how He could allow this. After all, He was the Son of God with all authority and power, so how could He allow that to happen? In their minds, those who have such power should be able to defeat their enemies every time! Jesus knew that God's way of battling and defeating the works of darkness was much different from that of men.

The account of the situation with James and John's mother is recorded in Mark 10:35-15 and in Matthew 20:20-28 (NLT):

> Then the mother of James and John, the sons of Zebedee, came to Jesus with her sons. She knelt respectfully to ask a favor. "What is your request?" he asked.
>
> She replied, "In your Kingdom, please let my two sons sit in places of honor next to you, one on your right and the other on your left." But Jesus answered by saying to them, "You don't know what you are asking! Are you able to drink from the bitter cup of suffering I am about to drink?"
>
> "Oh yes," they replied, "we are able!"
>
> Jesus told them, "You will indeed drink from my bitter cup. But I have no right to say who will sit on my right or my left. My Father has prepared those places for the ones he has chosen."
>
> When the ten other disciples heard what James and John had asked, they were indignant. But Jesus called them together and said, "You know that the rulers in this world lord it over their people, and officials flaunt their authority over those under them. But among you it will be different. Whoever wants to be a leader among you must be your servant, and whoever wants to be first among you must become your slave. For even the Son

## THE SECOND LESSON ON KINGDOM GREATNESS

of Man came not to be served but to serve others and to give his life as a ransom for many."

Mark records that it was John and James who asked, but Matthew says it was their mother. Whatever the case was, the source of the request had to have been John and James, even though their mother may have been the mouthpiece. Most likely, they were talking about it in front of their mother, and whether they asked their mother to ask Jesus, or their mother was just "being a mom" and trying to get the place for her sons doesn't matter; the underlying issue is still the same. She asked that they sit at the highest place of authority in Jesus' kingdom, which in their minds was like every other earthly kingdom that had ever been set up. Jesus' response is very interesting. He said, "You really don't know what you are asking." Jesus knew about His kingdom and how it would be very different than the earthly patterns the disciples had seen and heard about. He knew that to receive a very high place of authority, there had to be great amount of humility. In this case, the sacrifice Jesus talked about would end with them being tortured and possibly killed for their faith in Him.

The positions people were placed in to sit during Jesus' day had significance. Historically, when the Jews had a feast and set up tables, the event was set up in a square with one side left open. The person of highest authority would sit in the middle of the head table so they could see all the people around him. From there, people would sit to the left and to the right of the authority figure; your rank in authority was reflected by how close you sat to that person. The people directly to the right and to the left of the leader were the ones second and third in authority, whereas the people at the end of the tables—the far left and far right—were the people of lowest authority. John and James were going for broke and trying to out-maneuver the rest of their friends.

When the other ten disciples heard about this, they were very upset. I can picture them talking to themselves about the situation saying, "How could these two ask their mother to do this! What they really must have been mad about was that they had been out maneuvered by James and

John in trying to get a position in the kingdom. Like most of us, when situations like this happen, we go back and forth, not allowing other peoples' acts of selfish ambition get in our way. The disciples must have been dwelling on this and talking about it, so negative emotions and pride was probably taking over their thoughts and actions.

Our selfish ambition and desires will also blind us to the trials and problems of others. What the other disciples did not hear was that James and John would bear a similar fate as Jesus. Jesus already told them that He was going to the cross; He was going to be mistreated by the religious leaders one day and be killed. Selfishness blinds us to the plight of others and shuts off the compassion of God from working through us to help and strengthen others in their trials. In reality, selfish ambition that was encompassing the entire group of disciples was blinding them to the trials that Jesus was going to bear as well as the trials James and John were going to bear for being so close to Jesus. Jesus spoke explicitly to them about what was going to happen to Him, but they could not comprehend it; their hearts were blinded. We read the fulfillment of Jesus' words in Acts that James was put to death. And although John lived to a ripe old age, he was martyred for his faith.

The Lord's physical half-brother, James, weighs in on this subject in his epistle regarding jealousy and selfish ambition. James 3:16 (NLT) reads, **"Wherever there is jealousy and selfish ambition, there you will find disorder and evil of every kind**." James goes on to says that earthly wisdom is corrupted by sin and self-centeredness, describing the thinking that so pervaded the disciples' minds—it leads to all kinds of evil

The disciples decided to follow Jesus. They left all they had, and they pursued God—on the surface they had pure motives. The problem was that the surface does not expose the impurity that lies underneath. Just remember, before we judge the disciples, we need to understand that each of us would have struggled and been exposed the same way they were because we're all subject to the same frailties. We all need to have the same grace and mercy shown to us, so we can be transformed and changed the way they were.

James and John were transformed and changed. Jesus referred to them as "The Sons of Thunder." One day as I was praying with a friend, he told me that the Lord called me a "son of thunder." I thought, "Wow! This is a good thing. I must be a man of power and authority." So one day, I figured I should find out what that meant. I wasn't very pleased when I realized that "Sons of Thunder" meant "sons on tumults" and that James, John, and I were like bulls in a china closet! I went from thinking, "Wow, that's good" to, "Oh no, that's bad!" But if the power of God can change John from being a person who caused disruptions to become a disciple who was beloved of the Lord and a disciple of love, then there is hope for all of us. God's grace and mercy is enough to change and transform every human weakness and frailty into His image and likeness.

I am not sure how long the conversation and controversy of what James and John did go on as a topic of conversation between the disciples, but Jesus decided to address it again. He wanted the disciples to really understand that the principles of authority and honor work much differently in God's kingdom. He said that kings and those who are in authority want to flaunt their position before all who are around them. Like the centurion told Jesus in Matthew 8:8-9, people in authority want others to serve them. The centurion was a man with authority. He could command the people under him, and they would obey him. If they did not obey him, he could use his authority to punish them.

Jesus said that the rulers of the day would flaunt their authority. Have you ever heard anyone going up to someone else and asking, "Do you know who I am?" It's like making an announcement and saying, "I am so-and-so," as though it should impress and put awe and fear in us. Many times, these types of leaders use their authority to belittle and take advantage of people who serve them. Using their position, they can even physically and mentally abuse people.

In John's gospel (John 18:20-23), we see a situation like this where someone in authority is abusing their power. After Jesus is seized in the garden of Gethsemane, we read about Annas, one of the chief priests of the time, questioning Jesus and bringing false accusations against Him. When Jesus answered Annas, one of the officers struck Jesus for answering Annas disrespectfully or not answering the way they wanted. (Both thoughts can be argued.) But Jesus' answer pointed out their hypocrisy and their abuse of power. They were using their authority to physically abuse Jesus, in the process.

> Jesus answered him, "I have spoken openly to the world; I always taught in synagogues and in the temple, where all the Jews come together; and I spoke nothing in secret. "Why do you question me? Question those who have heard what I spoke to them; they know what I said." When He had said this, one of the officers standing nearby struck Jesus, saying, "Is that the way you answer the high priest?" Jesus answered him, "If I have spoken wrongly, testify of the wrong; but if rightly, why do you strike me?" (John 18:20-23).

When someone in authority wants you to know that they are in authority, they will tell you all the time. They usually do this because they are insecure and want to intimidate you to get what they want out of the situation. But Jesus never did that. He said, "I have come as a servant; I have come as a slave. I am here for your benefit. I am here to help you. I am here to make you better. I am here to make you the best you can be, not keep you under my thumb so you can serve me and my desires."

I like what Paul says in his first letter into the Corinthians. He told the members of the church at Corinth that they were fleshly and big babies because they were taking sides of the different leaders who would come and minister to them. Some were saying, "I am on Paul's side," and others, "I am on Apollos' side." We can easily say today, "I am a Protestant," or "I am a Catholic," or "I am from this church," I belong to that church." Paul sets the record straight by saying that we are simply servants of the Most High God. We each have a part, and each part we have causes growth in the kingdom, but God is the One who causes it all to grow and come together. Paul also knew that it was the grace of God that enabled him to do this. It was not his might or ability, but God's work in Him. He also knew that he would stand before the judgment seat of Christ someday, and his works as a servant in the body would be judged by the fire of God. The fire of God will expose all motives of selfishness, pride, and envy and show the true motives of what we do and why we do it. The works that we do because we love God and love people and serve them out of a pure heart—not for our own gain or notoriety—is like gold and will be a blessing to us in all eternity. The others will be consumed, and we could suffer loss of rewards before Him.

The greatest in the kingdom of God are those who, in meekness and humility, use their authority to help and build up people and are not concerned about personal gain or being served.

# THE THIRD LESSON ON KINGDOM GREATNESS

We can find even more insight about this issue the disciples were arguing over about being the greatest that Jesus was addressing in Luke 22:24-27. This time, the conversation happened right after the Passover meal, which wasn't too long after the mother of John and James came to Jesus asking for high positions of authority in the kingdom for her sons. Her request came right before Jesus' triumphant entry into Jerusalem.

They had just finished the Passover meal, and in Luke 22:15-20 we read:

> He said to them, "I have earnestly desired to eat this Passover with you before I suffer; for I say to you, I shall never again eat it **until it is fulfilled in the kingdom of God**," and when He had taken a cup and given thanks, He said, "Take this and share it among yourselves; for I say to you, **I will not drink of the fruit of the vine from now on until the kingdom of God comes**." And when He had taken some bread and given thanks, He broke it and gave it to them, saying, "This is my body which is given for you; do this in remembrance of me." And in the same way He took the cup after they had eaten, saying, "This cup which is poured out for you is the new covenant in my blood."

Jesus was telling them that He was going to suffer and that He would not eat with them again until the kingdom of God is fulfilled. So based on the disciples' thinking, the kingdom should be coming soon. As a matter of fact, the kingdom should be right around the corner, because it would come before they could have had another glass of wine together, which probably happened frequently, maybe every day or two! The disciples still did not understand the seriousness of the situation—that Jesus was about to be betrayed and was headed to His destiny, the cross. They had just heard that the kingdom was coming and thought only about the positions in the kingdom and how it would soon be divided.

You might ask why I am saying that about the disciples. We read in verse 24, "**And there arose also a dispute among them as to which one of them was regarded to be greatest**." Here is that the same old argument kicked up again! It happened at the Passover meal, right before Jesus was going to the garden of Gethsemane for prayer, just before the work of the cross was going to be consummated. Selfish ambition had so blinded the disciples that they really had no idea what was going to happen.

Jesus again went on to explain that their authority in the kingdom of God would not be like that of those in authority of their time. They were not to be like the kings of their time, who flaunted their authority and had others serve them. The disciples needed to understand that in Jesus' kingdom, to be great means that you serve, and to be great means that you don't lift yourself up, but you humble yourself. Jesus told them that in His kingdom, they shouldn't be the ones who sit at the dinner table looking to get the seat closest to the king, but they should be the ones who serve the people at the table. In His kingdom, they shouldn't be telling people that they have authority and brag about their position, but instead they should be asking people how they can help and serve them.

Not only did Jesus discuss this same topic again, but He demonstrated it by preforming the lowest job a servant would do. If you look at the timeline of the Gospels, John records that Jesus laid aside His garment, took a towel, girded himself as a servant, took a basin, and washed the

## THE THIRD LESSON ON KINGDOM GREATNESS

disciples' feet. John records that He did this right after the Passover meal. Peter starts to argue with Jesus again as Jesus washed their feet. Peter said, "You cannot do this! This is not the job of Christ the King, the leader of the kingdom!" It probably sounded noble for Peter to say such a thing, but he still had not grasped the kingdom version of the "greatest." Jesus, as patient as ever, told Peter, "If you don't let me wash your feet, you will have no part with me." His response can also be translated as Peter would have no position in the kingdom. Peter wanted that position so badly that he said, "Lord, wash all of me then!" Jesus finished performing the humblest act and service to His disciples, thus demonstrating His kingdom's version of greatness.

We all know that it is not uncommon for those who are in authority to use their authority—whether maliciously or non-maliciously—to affect people under their authority either positively or negatively. People who have authority can use their power to manipulate, control, and make others' lives difficult, or they can use their power to benefit others. Most in authority are "mixed bags," meaning that they have both helped and hurt—some for selfish reasons, some for reasons not known, and some for reasons of ignorance.

I think people gravitate to power and authority because it makes them feel that they have control in their lives. This authority we have allows us to control our circumstances. It allows us to be and do more than we can do on our own. We like power and authority because it makes us feel important and good about who we are. Usually this comes from those under us telling us how good we are or how well we do things. These people will probably never criticize us because they are afraid of our reaction and what we may do to them as a result of their feedback.

Jesus wanted to give the disciples a principle of the kingdom that would allow them to walk in authority and always be right about their motives and actions. That no matter what they did, they would be using their authority for the benefit of others. This principle was being a servant, not seeking how people could serve them because of their position, but seeking how they could serve others with the authority they had in order to help and benefit them.

This is how Jesus came—as a servant. Let's put this in perspective. He is the second person of the Trinity. Paul describes that Jesus existed as God in Philippians 2:6, but regarded equality with God as something He should not cling to. Let me describe this in another way: Jesus was God, but being equal to God was not the thing He prized above all things; and although this was the highest place of authority, He was willing to shed that glory. So if Jesus didn't count being equal to God as the highest prize, what did He regard as the highest prize? He regarded doing the will of the Father and redeeming man as the highest prize. Think of it, God regarded us as the ultimate prize and became a man—He became His very creation. When He became a man, He came as a king arrayed in man's dusty glory. He humbled Himself as a servant.

As I finish these discussions about who is the greatest, I want us all to understand that all of us, to a certain degree, would have the same weakness and frailties that the disciples had. In retrospect, it's easy to think how weak and stupid they were as we read these accounts and conversations, and we may think the same things that we think of the sin of Adam and Eve: "How could they do what they did?" They lived in the presence of God; they were without a corrupted sin nature. But they did sin—*and we all would have done the same thing!* Until we come to that revelation we will, to some degree, live in deception. Our level of deception is determined based on how differently we may see and judge things from God's perspective.

Oh, how the disciples came to understand these principles as they grew and matured in spiritual things! I think of Peter who wrote some wonderful, inspirational passages in his letters that all point to a deep understanding of these truths.

I expounded on 1 Peter 2:1-2 in an earlier chapter. Peter went even further than saying, "Become like a little child." He said, "Become even more dependent on God by acting like a newborn babe." He said, "Put aside

## THE THIRD LESSON ON KINGDOM GREATNESS

envy and become like a baby who needs his mother's milk to survive." It was pride that led to envy and jealously, which was what fueled the conversation about who was the greatest, and Peter had matured to the point that he was far from those "evil cousins."

In 1 Peter 5 we also read Peter's wonderful exhortation to leaders about how to shepherd the flock of God. He says not to force them or manipulate them to get money out of them, but to be an example. He told them to be an example that is not a show, but an example that is a life in union with Jesus, walking in humility as a leader. And although Peter exhorts people to submit to leaders in humility, he also knew this was a two-way street—leaders need to submit to their people as well. Just as Jesus clothed himself to be a servant and washed their feet, Peter said that we are to be clothed and covered in humility because God opposes the proud. He learned that God stands resolutely against the proud but gives grace to the humble. Jesus said that he who humbles himself will be exalted.

# PRINCIPLE 3: KINGDOM POWER

Jesus knew that He was going to set up a kingdom. This kingdom was going to be different from what everyone expected, including His disciples. He knew that their motives were at times corrupt and not pure, but Jesus did not get uptight about it, instead He kept instructing them in the proper motives and attitudes of leaders in the kingdom. He knew that He needed to sow the word and to accomplish His ministry on the earth. He also knew that upon His death and resurrection the Holy Spirit was going to come and live in them to take the word sowed into them and transform them as people in the kingdom of God

We are going to go through two stories which have very deep truths regarding true kingdom authority.

The first one I want to bring up is found in Luke 10:1-16. In this story, Jesus sends seventy of his followers out, telling them the harvest is plenty, but the laborers are few. Among other things, He instructs them to heal the sick because the kingdom of God is near.

They go out and later come back pretty pumped up because not only did they heal the sick, but they were able to cast out demons like Jesus did. Remember how astonished everyone was in the beginning of Jesus' ministry when He would cast demons out of people. Now they were doing the same thing, with the same power and authority Jesus did. The demons were subject to them in His name, and they cast them out just like He did.

I remember the first few times I was confronted by a person who was under the influence of an evil spirit. I got pretty pumped up also. I was in my senior year in college, and a bunch of us met at a local church for prayer. As we held hands and started to pray, I saw a sister in the Lord across from me, and in my spirit, I sensed that she was being choked, like something was grabbing her around the neck. So in the middle of prayer I walked over to her and told her that the Lord wanted me to pray for her. She consented. I then asked another friend of mine who was a bodybuilder to get behind her. I felt like the Lord wanted to do something for her, so I wanted him to catch her if she fell under the power of God. He reluctantly got behind her, thinking nothing was going to happen. As I laid my hands on her, she fell like she'd gotten hit in the head with a brick. My bodybuilder-buddy almost got knocked over and hardly had the strength to catch her. As she was on the ground, I went near her again, and said, "You spirit of fear and anxiety, leave her alone and come out of her." She then started pounding her legs, and—in a different voice—said, "We don't want to come out." I commanded them in the name of Jesus to leave. The sister sat up and was free; the Spirit of the Lord filled the place. My bodybuilder friend was running all over the platform of the church and praising God. We were all rejoicing for what the Lord did for our sister. So I understand what it felt like for the disciples when they came back to Jesus!

After this incident, we would often go out to certain nearby towns at night (which were not the best places to be in), and witness to people and cast out demons. We used to exchange "demon casting out" stories. One time, as a friend and I (who is now a senior pastor in a large church) were walking around witnessing to people, we came across a guy who was working at a parking garage. We started witnessing to him and eventually led him to the Lord. We prayed and asked God to fill him with the Holy Spirit. As we were praying, the guy said that he was seeing a light in the room. He started acting erratically, rubbing his hands together and saying he was thirsty. He then abruptly got up

## PRINCIPLE 3: KINGDOM POWER

and went to the bathroom to get a drink. As he was walking away, I remembered scriptures where Jesus talked about how when demons are cast out, they go into dry and waterless places. I also remembered a teaching I heard from a man who used to do a lot of deliverance. He said that many times people would call out for water in the middle of deliverance. He would joke that the devil is always thirsty, probably because of the place he and the demons live and are going to end up forever. I followed the guy into the bathroom and started to cast the devil out of him. As I kept saying, "In the name of Jesus, come out of him," he stiffened up like a board and then—boom! He fell over and hit the tile floor like a dead weight. He just lay there—out cold. Not sure if it was the deliverance or how hard he hit the tile (probably a little of both). At that point, I looked at my friend and he asked me, "What should we do now?" I said, "I don't know." We just left the guy there, out cold on the tile floor of the bathroom, and left. I often wondered what he thought when he woke up. One thing I know is that, whatever evil power was influencing him was gone and that he was delivered! We were pumped. We had just done some devil hunting, and I am sure God did something in that guy. But I think our motives were a little off. We were like western gunslingers looking for a devil fight. But we did have power and authority to cast out demons.

Now, getting back to our topic on Jesus talking to His disciples (and me), He told them that He saw Satan fall from heaven like lighting. He told them not to rejoice that evil is subject to His name, but rather rejoice over their names being written in the Book of Life.

Part of the story of Lucifer's fall from heaven can be found in Isaiah 14 and Ezekiel 28:

Isaiah 14:12-15 says:

> "How you have fallen from heaven,
> O star of the morning, son of the dawn!
> You have been cut down to the earth,
> You who have weakened the nations!

> "But you said in your heart,
> 'I will ascend to heaven;
> I will raise my throne above the stars of God,
> And I will sit on the mount of assembly
> In the recesses of the north.
> 'I will ascend above the heights of the clouds;
> I will make myself like the Most High.'
> "Nevertheless you will be thrust down to Sheol,
> To the recesses of the pit.

Pride was found in Lucifer because of his beauty. He was the morning star that covered the throne of God. He was of the highest rank of angels, but when pride was found in him and he rebelled against God, he was thrown down from the highest position of any created being in heaven, and God sent him to hell.

Lighting moves at around 186,000 miles per second, which is the speed of light. That's how fast pride can bring us down. Jesus was warning the disciples not to rejoice in the power and authority that He gave them. Pride can be an enough reason for every human failure and fault. It brings us to a place where we think power and authority comes from us and that we are special. That will always get us into a place of self-deception.

It amazes me to see how quickly pride can be found in us. Remember Saul, the first-appointed king of Israel? He was timid and afraid of being a king over Israel. He was hiding when they were looking for him to take his throne. God's anointing came on him and the Bible tells us that he became "another man," in the good, godly sense of the word. But it wasn't long after that when he started ignoring the prophet and the word of God and did what *he* thought was right. That was the beginning of the end of Saul. He lost course and never finished the plan of God for his life. He became a controlling, manipulative leader and died an untimely death.

## PRINCIPLE 3: KINGDOM POWER

It can be the beginning of the end for all of us. How many well-meaning and anointed men and woman of God in recent history have succumbed to this same thing? They start out humble and small, begin to have success in ministry, and the anointing of the Spirit of God comes upon them, and healings, miracles, and other manifestations of the Spirit happen through them. They start to get notoriety, and suddenly humility diminishes, and they succumb to pride and deception about their own importance. They forget that what they have is because of the grace of God. Then anointed person you see in the pulpit is not the same person in "real life." They act one way in public and a live a secret life of sin and despair in private.

I have learned that our measure of spirituality is not gauged by what people see us do in public; it is measured by what God and those who know us best see us do in private. The ministry gift that is given to us for the benefit of the body of Christ does not do anything for us in our private communion with God. We all need to establish a personal communion with God in private, and this will keep our direction and motivation in the right track for our public ministry.

Jesus was warning the disciples of this when He said (and I paraphrase), "Don't rejoice that you have power to cast out demons, and don't rejoice that you can heal the sick or that the power of the Holy Spirit works through you. Rejoice greatly that you are saved by the grace of God; that it is not of yourselves, but that from God, and God alone, your name is written in the book of life. Spend more time in your fellowship with God, than you do recounting the miracles and works that God does through you."

I was listening to a minister teaching a group of young people. He was quite older than them, probably in his late 50s, and was commenting that he had heard a lot of younger ministers say that they want all of God they can get—but he said that he didn't. That caught my attention. I was one of those young people. I wanted all of God that I could get. The minister went on to say, "I only want as much of God as I can handle at one point in time." He realized that when God puts His glory on you and the power works through you, people will see that, and you will be tempted—just like Balaam and many men of God have been—to merchandize the anointing. This minister wanted to make sure his heart was right before God, and not think that any of this was by himself, but by God, and give all the glory to Him. This minister knew the weaknesses of the flesh. He was more interested in the power to transform himself into the image and likeness of God than the power to work though him and bring healing and miracles that would bring attention to him.

When our goal is to be more known of and by God than to be known as a "man of God," our motives get purified by Him. Ultimately, it is all about knowing God and communing with God—and nobody sees that but God.

I was talking to another pastor friend on a similar subject and was reiterating a story that happened to me. I was teaching one Sunday morning, filling in for the senior pastor for two services. I thought the teaching went well; the presence of God was there, and the message was flowing. After the first service I got off the stage and walked to meet and greet people. The Lord stopped me in my tracks and said, "What are you doing? The reason you came out is to hear people commend you on your message. Go back into the office and wait for the next service to start." OOUCH! That hurt! But it was true. I was exulting more in the anointing working through me and was enjoying being commended for it, rather than rejoicing that my name was written in the book of life.

Sometime later, I was reading about A.W. Tozer, a man of God, a pastor who was well known for his revelatory teachings, and an author of many wonderful books. He said that when he finished teaching on Sundays, he would never go out and greet the people leaving church. He said that he did not want to get deceived by the complements he would get on his teaching ability. He did not want the commendation of man, which can easily deceive. He wanted the commendation and communion of God. I am not saying that we as pastors should not greet people, but that was a personal conviction he had, one which helped his perspective to be right before God.

## PRINCIPLE 3: KINGDOM POWER

In my early 20s, I felt a strong call of God on my life, but God did not allow me to go to Bible school. So I started studying by myself. I read hundreds of books and would study the Bible all the time. Once or twice a month I would go away for two days and stay in a hotel to pray, fast, study, and seek God. I fasted so much and wore my body down that I got mononucleosis. In retrospect, the way I wore my body down was not a wise thing to do, but I needed to get the anointing so I could fulfill my ministry. One day I realized that I was doing this more for the anointing in my life so God could work through me with His power. I was rejoicing more in the power than I was rejoicing in God.

Have you ever wondered why Jesus told the people He ministered to not to tell anybody who healed them after they were healed or delivered from a demon? Look at the following instances: the leper in Matthew 8, the blind man in Matthew 9, and the young girl Jesus raised from the dead in Mark 5. The question is: Why did Jesus tell them not to do this? I am sure there was more than one reason, but I think one of the reasons is that Jesus was more concerned about doing the will of God and finishing the task that God the Father sent Him to do rather than the popularity and notoriety that would have come with people knowing.

He knew that when people heard about the miracles, they would be seeking Him everywhere, and it would be easy for Him to get distracted from listening to the Father regarding His mission on earth. Jesus said, "I only do what I see the Father do." Jesus accomplished what He did because that was what He saw the Father doing. In His ministry, Jesus would pull away from the crowds and pray. There were times when it was difficult to travel because of His popularity. Wherever Jesus went, people wanted to hear Him and see healings and miracles happen. On the other hand, wherever He went, religious leaders were trying to take Him down because of their jealousy and pride. The point I am getting to here is when the power of God flows through us and miracles happen, it can become easy for the notoriety and popularity to start driving our motives regarding what we do and how we do it, rather than doing things because it is what we see the Father doing through us. I know we should testify of the things God does for us, but we need to be careful that the power working through us does not corrupt our motives and change how we interact with God and people.

The issue that we run into here, to some degree or another, is that we allow the desire to receive honor and glory for the work that God has done through us. Although we know this isn't good, the weakness of the flesh comes in. We feel accepted by God and man; by God because He did such a work through us and we feel validated by him, and by man because we receive honor and recognition for the power working through us, and people start to esteem us, our ministry, our calling, and our position in the body.

The problem we run into is when God wants us to do something that is contrary to what people want. Jesus ran into this all the time. He would gather a crowd and say something that did not sit well with people based on their current doctrine or understanding of God. We read about one such instance in John 6 when Jesus fed five-thousand people through a miracle. This got peoples' attention and they were saying that Jesus was "the prophet" who they were expecting to come into the world. Jesus knew that the people were esteeming Him and wanted to make Him king. Later that day Jesus sent His disciples across the sea, and when they were troubled, He walked on water to get to them and He saved them. What a day's work of miracles: feeding the five-thousand, walking on water, and stopping a storm—that's a nice day of ministry!

Once people saw that Jesus was gone, they followed Him in their small boats, still seeking Him. As soon as they got to where Jesus was, rather than tickling their ears to gain more followers, Jesus tells them that they only seek Him because their stomachs were filled. He challenges them to seek the food that leads to eternal life. Jesus goes on to say that He is the bread of life. The Jews and the people were perplexed at this and many who had been following Him left at this point. Jesus was not motivated by the honor of people or crowds. He was motivated by doing the will of the Father. When we are motivated by the honor of people, we will do things that bring us more honor, even when we know it may

## PRINCIPLE 3: KINGDOM POWER

run against the will of God. Then our judgment gets clouded because we are motivated by self rather than by God.

In John 5:44, Jesus asks, "How can you believe, when you receive glory from one another, and you do not seek the glory that is from the one and only God?" This is a very interesting and insightful exposition of what happens to us when we seek honor and power that leads us to the desire for glory and honor for ourselves. Jesus said that we cannot believe; if that is the case, how can we walk with true faith in God? The scriptures say without faith it is impossible to please God. If we aren't walking in faith, we end up having to find an alternative way to sustain our ministry, which usually turns into hyping things up, trusting in our natural abilities, and drawing people to ourselves rather than drawing people to God.

I realize that there is a very fine line here. When we learn just to rejoice in who God is, what He saved us from, where has He brought us to, and know all things are from Him and for Him, it keeps us in a place of humility and trust in God that will allow us to walk down the straight and narrow way. It helps us to stand before the judgment seat of Christ. *Then* we can be commended for our works and rejoice in our God, rather than be in a place of suffering loss, where Jesus has to wipe away our tears because we finally see the true motives and results of our self-influenced works and the loss of intended rewards that He so wants to give us.

# PART 3: MASTER BUILDER PRINCIPLES 4-7—BECOMING AN OVERCOMER

# PRINCIPLE 4: OVERCOMING INSECURITY AND REJECTION

In this chapter I want to deal with commonly-faced issues that most men and women deal with. Unless checked, submitted, and transformed by the grace of God, these issues can cause us to act in ways that are quite opposite to God's ways—even when we have the best intentions to serve God. These two issues are insecurity and rejection. Generally, rejection of some sort leads to insecurity regarding who we are and the position God has put us in. When insecurity creeps into us, we will try to find a way to "secure" who we are.

When it comes to business and politics, if someone is challenging our position and authority, we usually find a way to overcome that challenge. We can either do that in a way that shows truth and reveals why we are doing what we are doing, or we can do that in a way that will discredit our challenger and undermine them in ways that are malicious. Normally this is done by destroying reputations, making up fictitious stories, taking things out of context, and doing whatever we can do to shore up our position—whatever is done is for one's own benefit at the expense of others. The root of this is selfishness, which is evil, and the opposite of good. We know this because goodness will motivate us to do things for the benefit of others even at our own expense. This can happen in the church when someone's authority is challenged based on their decisions, position, or actions. Rather than allowing the facts to speak for themselves and for God's righteous judgment, we try to discredit the person by pointing out their shortcomings and issues and distorting the issues to our benefit. Generally, we try to destroy the reputation of someone else so we can maintain our position. This method of behavior started back in the garden of Eden when Adam first perpetrated it. God asked Adam why he and Eve ate of the Tree of the Knowledge of Good and Evil. Adam blamed God and Eve saying, "It was the woman you gave me who made me eat it." He tried to secure his position, rather than admitting his fault and frailty, which was made plain by not exercising his God-given authority over the garden to "guard and keep it."

The religious leaders of Jesus' day did that too. Rather than accepting the truths Jesus was speaking, which challenged the religious order of their time, they tried to find fault with Jesus so they could accuse Him, discredit Him, and find some way to bring Him down. Any method was open for consideration, even using people. We can see this in the story of the woman caught in adultery. The religious leaders were willing to have the woman stoned in order to find fault with Jesus. These leaders were insecure in their position and wanted to do anything they could to maintain their authority and power in the current structure. They twisted the truth in every way to their advantage.

The Jewish religious leaders did the same to Jesus when they apprehended Him before His crucifixion. They had people come before them and testify about Him, but nothing seemed to "stick" to Jesus. When they asked Him to reply to their testimonies, Jesus said, "I spoke openly in public…There was nothing in secret…Just ask the people who were around and listened." Because they couldn't find fault with Him through the accusations, they tried to intimidate Him with physical abuse. When the religious leaders brought Jesus before Pilate, he found no wrong in Him. But they pressured Pilate until he folded. They did anything they could to make sure Jesus was put to death and their perceived position was preserved. The religious leaders also did this to Paul when he was preaching about Jesus being the Messiah.

Before we indict any one leader or person, we need to understand that the same tendencies work in all of us. Unless we have grace and are

## PRINCIPLE 4: OVERCOMING INSECURITY AND REJECTION

willing to look at the truth, given the right circumstances, we all might be guilty of the same thing.

In the gospel of Luke we read a story about an entire group of people who were rejected. Jesus was headed to Jerusalem for the final part of His earthly mission. Usually the shortest way to travel to Jerusalem from North Israel was to travel through Samaria. Rather than going through Samaria, most Jews would walk around Samaria to get to Jerusalem. Why did they do this? Because the Samaritans were considered half-breeds and not true Jews. Although the Samaritans worshipped God, the Jews did not want to be "polluted" by associating with them. They considered it righteous to dissociate with them. This segregation went on for years. Tension between the two groups arose. The rejection of the Samaritans by the Jews was always in the forefront of their thinking. Prejudice was being passed down from generation to generation on both sides of that cultural divide.

From what is recorded in the Gospels, we read that Jesus did not feel or act that way. We see that through the parable of the Good Samaritan and the story of the Samaritan woman at the well.

Let's take a look at the story of the woman at the well. Jesus was passing through and came to Jacob's well. The disciples left Jesus to get something to eat and while they were gone, Jesus started a conversation with a Samaritan woman. This woman was the "rejected of the rejected" for her time. First, she was a woman. Second, she was a Samaritan. Third, she was rejected even by the Samaritans. The reason I say that is because she was out drawing water from the well at midday by herself. Most women went out early in the morning to draw water because it was cooler. Most likely, she was looked down upon because of her sordid and loose past. Jesus tells her that He is thirsty and asks for water. Although He thirsted for natural water, He also thirsted for fellowship with her—to reveal who He was to her. He ministered to her, and as the conversation progressed, He plainly told her that He was the Messiah who the Samaritans were looking for. It is not recorded in the Gospels anywhere else that Jesus was as direct and straight forward with anyone else about His eternal identity.

That woman who had been married to or living with six successive men, finally met the real bridegroom, Jesus, who was the seventh—and the perfect—one. The Samaritan woman came to the well to draw water and received living water that was springing up in her—wells of everlasting life. She was so excited that she ran and told all the people in the town. She was the first Samaritan evangelist! It is recorded that the people of the city came out to see Jesus because of that woman's words, and after hearing and seeing Him, they believed in Him (John 4:39-42). Jesus stayed there with them for two days. The scriptures don't record all that Jesus said or did, but I'm sure it made an impact on the region, and many of the people who heard him speak were healed and delivered.

Just think how much this would have impacted the social and spiritual norms of the times! Jesus went to Samaria and stayed there for two days. This must have gotten to the ears of the Jewish people and the Jewish religious leaders. It did not help Jesus' popularity with them. Maybe that is why in John 8 they were accusing Jesus of being a Samaritan and—even worse—a demon-possessed Samaritan. The Samaritans must have been overjoyed that Jesus spent time with them, and He must have been held in high esteem. Long-standing prejudices ran deep, and Jesus was running headfirst into some major ones by doing what He did.

It is not recorded in the scriptures that Jesus went into Samaria after this, but that does not mean He didn't. Because the gospel accounts are only select moments in time over a three-year period, the apostle John said that if all that Jesus said and did were to be recorded during that time, the whole world could not contain the books that could be written (John 21:25).

There was one last encounter with the Samaritans as Jesus was ending His earthy ministry. He was heading toward Jerusalem for the Passover, as many Jews did. Jesus could have done the traditional, prejudicial thing and gone around Samaria like everyone else had done. Not Jesus.

PRINCIPLE 4: OVERCOMING INSECURITY AND REJECTION

Instead, He sent word ahead that He was coming through Samaria because He had already established a relationship with them. He added that He was not going to stop and minister to them, but instead was going to pass through to go straight to Jerusalem. When the Samaritans heard about that, they told Him not to come. It is apparent that even with Jesus doing what He did for them, old hurts and prejudices did not die quickly. Jesus was rejected and disrespected by the Samaritans even after accepting them and treating them with respect and dignity, something no other Jew of that time had done. Let's read the account that Luke records:

> When the days were approaching for His ascension, He was determined to go to Jerusalem; And He sent messengers on ahead of Him, and they went and entered a village of the Samaritans to make arrangements for Him. But they did not receive Him, because He was traveling toward Jerusalem. When His disciples James and John saw this, they said, "Lord, do you want us to command fire to come down from heaven and consume them?" But He turned and rebuked them, [and said, "You do not know what kind of spirit you are of; for the Son of Man did not come to destroy men's lives, but to save them."] And they went on to another village (Luke 9:51-56).

When James and John, the "Sons of Thunder" (or in other words, the "Sons of Tumults") were suggesting making some mayhem, they were angry because they were all disrespected and rejected. Any strong worldly leader of the day would have shown the Samaritans that this would not be tolerated and that someone would have to pay for such an act. They came up with a wonderful way of doing this to show them never to disrespect Jesus again. They said, "Let's burn them to a crisp and expect judgment from heaven. They are just Samaritans anyway." But that's not how Jesus operated.

When I think of fire coming down from heaven, I think of the people of Sodom and Gomorrah, who God judged for their sins and consumed the entire cities with fire. In all of history, something like this is recorded just once. The depth of sin there must have been so great for a God who would rather show mercy than judgment, to destroy an entire population. The question is why James and John would want to initiate such a judgment like this on the Samaritans.

James and John were acting as worldly authority would act. They thought that because they were going to be leaders in the kingdom of Jesus, they had to lead with a strong hand and authority. Later in the Gospels, we see Jesus dealing with this and explaining to them as to how they were not to act like the worldly authorities and leaders. Jesus said, "You don't know what spirit you are of." That is a question we should ask ourselves at times like this, especially if we are dealing with rejection and hurt.

In this last Samaritan pass-through, Jesus and His disciples were rejected. James and John were probably thinking, "Don't they remember how we came and ministered to them, stayed with them, and showed them compassion and acceptance like no other Jews before. They have no understanding about the criticism we got for joining them and going to Samaria. How could they reject us now? They need to understand the magnitude of what they did and the ramifications that should come from this."

All these things were true, but that didn't give James and John the right to be a judge and executioner. Jesus decided not to allow the hurt and rejection they were acting out to cause Him to act the same way. Jesus understood the history in the region and how mercilessly the Samaritans were treated by the Jews. He knew the practice of the day that many Jews would rather walk around Samaria to go to Jerusalem and take a much longer journey rather than go through Samaria. He knew Jews commonly called them dogs. When the Samaritans rejected Jesus, He did not want to bring judgment. He had mercy, because He knew the source of their hurt and He had a much greater work to accomplish.

Jesus also knew that after His work on the cross and the outpouring of the Holy Spirit, the gospel would be preached in Judea, Samaria, and to

## PRINCIPLE 4: OVERCOMING INSECURITY AND REJECTION

the uttermost parts of the earth. He knew that once God poured out His Spirit and access was provided to the kingdom, man's heart would be changed and transformed Jesus could then work with the deep-seated rejections and resentments the have been embedded there for eons.

If Jesus was concerned about vindicating a wrong and executing judgment on the Samaritans, He would have never fulfilled God's purposes in His life. Being motivated by a spirit of rejection will cause us to make decisions and take actions that will be far from the will of God; taking us on a negative course that we would have never imagined we could get into. James and John wanting to ask Jesus to call fire down from heaven is an example of this. Any leader in either small or large groups will always be presented with a situation of rejection. Usually it takes the form of criticism. It amazes me how much diametrically opposed feedback a leader can get from people on the same subject. One person can praise what you are doing while the other person is ripping it apart.

How we react to the situation is critically important. Do we try to find fault with that person? Do we try to find a way to discredit that person? Do we try to tear down that person? Today we have so many media outlets; we can let the world know many things in matter of seconds, and the temptation is strong to just post a rant—don't do it!

As we think about the situation or person, we need to ask ourselves what kind of spirit we are acting out of. Are we being led by God's Spirit, or are we allowing evil to lead our wounded soul and get comfort and vindication for ourselves? Are we operating out of a spirit of meekness, or are we operating out of a spirit of pride? I like to define meekness as "power (authority) under control, submitted to the will of God." Paul makes the point very well in Galatians 6:

> Brethren, even if anyone is caught in any trespass, you who are spiritual, restore such a one in a spirit of gentleness (meekness); each one looking to yourself, so that you too will not be tempted. Bear one another's burdens, and

> thereby fulfill the law of Christ. For if anyone thinks he is something when he is nothing, he deceives himself. But each one must examine his own work, and then he will have reason for boasting in regard to himself alone, and not in regard to another (Galatians 6:1-4).

I have been in situations both as a willing and unwilling participant (unfortunately), where someone criticized another, which led to a systematic destruction of the person who was criticized. Information gets fed about a person to other people, knowing it will get around and discredit someone. Every time we do this, we lessen our authority in the kingdom of God, taking authority and judgment to ourselves. We take vindication in our own hands and leave God out of the equation.

These types of sharp criticism are a quick path to short-circuiting the authority and power of God in our lives and blinding our spiritual eyesight. This reminds me of what Jesus was talking about in Matthew 7. The Lord gave me a revelation on this years ago while I was in a worship service, minding my own business. The Holy Spirit interrupted my worship with a revelation. If we are sensitive to Him, the Holy Spirit will often do this. Worship many times will lead to revelation from God. I think this should be a common practice, because when we focus on Him and worship Him for Who He is, He reveals Himself to us.

Regarding judgement, the Lord took me to Matthew 7 and opened my eyes to show me how guilty I was of judging. Then I saw how that type of attitude just short-circuited the presence and power of God in my life. Let's read what Jesus said in Barclay's translation:

> Do not judge others, in order that you may not be judged; for with the standard of judgment with which you judge you will be judged; and with the measure you measure to others it will be measured to you. Why do you **look for the speck of dust** in your brother's eye, and never notice the plank that is in your own eye? Or, how will you say to your brother: "Let me remove the speck of dust in

## PRINCIPLE 4: OVERCOMING INSECURITY AND REJECTION

your eye," and, see, there is a plank in your eye; **then you will see clearly to remove the speck of dust from your brother's eye** (Matthew 7:1).

After the Lord took me to the scripture and gave me an understanding of it, I started spending time meditating on it. Sometimes we do a disservice when the Holy Spirit starts to reveal scripture to us and then we never spend time in His presence meditating and studying what we perceive the Lord is showing us. I have always found that there is more to the revelations the Lord gives me if I will just take some time to seek His face in a deeper and more deliberate manner.

The word *judge* has a deeper meaning here. It means "to assume the office of a judge; to undergo the process of trial and to sentence; to condemn and execute judgment upon." This type of judgement is a habit of harsh unjust criticism. The English word *critic* is derived from the Greek word *krinein*.

The scripture says that we look at the speck in our brother's eye. But we do more than just a cursory look. We direct our mind, we contemplate, and we examine that speck very carefully. Why is it we always notice the shortcomings and sins of other people? Sometimes we say that we are just "discerning," but what we do with that discernment and how we act on it will determine whether we act like a loving father or a roaring lion who wants to devour its prey. The scripture also goes on to says that we do not consider the plank in our own eyes, meaning that we don't ponder our own shortcomings.

Let's draw an analogy between the speck and the beam. The speck is a piece of dried wood, a splinter, or a very small particle that can irritate. There is something there that needs to be cut out and taken care of. The beam is like a main rafter in a house that holds up the roof. So obviously there is a great difference here.

This is what the Lord showed me. Many times when we see a fault in a brother, rather than gently trying to remove a small splinter from his eye, we take the sword of the Spirit (which is the Word of God) and cut his head off. You know what? The splinter isn't there anymore, but the person is beat up and bloodied by the incident, and it takes months to heal. I call this the Samurai method. We show no compassion, mercy, or meekness—and we ourselves can be overtaken with the same fault. We are usually more interested in showing them their faults. This could be for many reasons. It could be because we want to prove ourselves right and them wrong; it could be because we want to put the light on their fault and not our own. Maybe it is a way we can control them and exercise superiority over them. Or it might be a way of getting back at them because we were offended by them. The key is that love should always desire to build up and restore, not tear down, control, or belittle.

The Pharisees looked to tear down, control, or belittle. Think about the situation when they brought the woman caught in adultery to Jesus (John 8:1-11). Were their motives to bring righteous judgment to the situation, or to use the woman to catch Jesus in a question about the law? The result would have been the death of Jesus and the woman. The Pharisees would have been fine with this because it would have allowed them to remain in control. But Jesus knew the motivation of their hearts and diffused the situation, making them look at their own sin before they could condemn the woman for her sin.

Another thing we do that reveals our impure motives is to manipulate the truth to better serve our purposes. The scriptures say that both the woman and the man who committed adultery should be brought for judgment. But where was the man? For all we know, the Pharisees knew exactly where to find this woman because the woman may have been a prostitute and they may have used her services. So if they knew where *she* was, they would have known where *he* was!

When people are under a religious spirit, they manipulate the whole truth or partial truth to serve their purposes. That is what the devil tried to do when he quoted scriptures to Jesus in Matthew 4 during Jesus' temptation in the wilderness. But Jesus knew the spirit of the law, the heart of the Father, and not the letter of the law. He spoke the pure truth

## PRINCIPLE 4: OVERCOMING INSECURITY AND REJECTION

of the Word; the devil could not have any control or power over the pure Word of God.

To finish the revelation, the Lord showed me how I did this to a good friend who was going through an emotionally difficult time. I knew that my friend was not making decisions in his own best interest. He would not listen to anyone. I got frustrated with him and just blasted him. Do you think he listened to me? No, he didn't. As a matter of fact, it hurt our relationship and limited my ability to speak into his life. I was more concerned about him understanding that I was right and that he was wrong, than me understanding the hurt which was causing him to make such unwise decisions. I was more interested in proving myself right than helping him. I was acting just like the Pharisees. The beam in my eye was the lack of mercy, compassion, and understanding. Just because we speak the truth doesn't mean it is in love. We can speak the truth, and it can hurt people unnecessarily. It all comes down to the motivation of our heart. In the end, what this situation did to me was lessened the true heavenly authority in my life. The results were from earthly wisdom, not heavenly wisdom.

The Lord spoke to me and reminded me that when I judge and correct others I need to be like a master surgeon. The object of a good surgeon is to take away the defective area or repair it without disturbing or hurting the surrounding tissues so the person can recover faster with the least amount of pain. Just think: prior to the 1990s, when someone was to have knee surgery for cartilage repair, the surgeon had to make a large incision in the knee to get to the cartilage. As a result, the recovery time to full strength was usually many months. But now we have arthroscopic techniques which can do the same repairs very quickly and without damage to other surrounding tissues. The recovery time is usually three or four weeks. It's that kind of precision with which we need to prayerfully discern and admonish loving correction.

I like what Matthew Henry says in his commentary about sharp judgment. We must not judge rashly, nor pass such a judgment upon our brother as has no ground, but is only the product of our own jealousy and ill nature.

We must not make the worst of people, nor infer such insidious things from their words and actions as they will not bear. We must not judge uncharitably, unmercifully, nor with a spirit of revenge, and a desire to do mischief. We must not judge of a man's state by a single act, nor of what he is in himself by what he is to us, because in our own cause we are apt to be partial. We must not judge the hearts of others, nor their intentions, for it is God's prerogative to try the heart, and we must not step into his throne; nor must we judge of their eternal state, nor call them *hypocrites, reprobates*, and *castaways;* that is stretching beyond our line; what have we to do, thus to judge another man's servant? Counsel him, and help him, but do not judge him.[1]

I want to get back to the point I made in chapter 3 when I referred to Matthew 18:1-6 where the disciples were fighting over who was the greatest. Jesus brought a little child to them, and in His explanation, He said to them that unless they act like a little child, they will not even get into the kingdom, much less have a position in it.

I love how Peter got his revelation later in the New Testament! It is so clearly stated in 1 Peter 2:1-2:

> Therefore, **putting aside all malice and all deceit and hypocrisy and envy and all slander,** like **newborn babies**, long for the pure milk of the word, so that by it you may grow in respect to salvation.

James writes something very similar in James 1:21:

> Therefore, putting aside all filthiness and all that remains of wickedness (malice), in humility receive the word implanted, which is able to save your souls.

If we allow this spirit of rejection to work in us, it will allow our insecurities to lead us to acts of malice, which will lead us to envy and

---

1. Henry, M. (1994). *Matthew Henry's commentary on the whole Bible: complete and unabridged in one volume* (p. 1643). Peabody: Hendrickson.

## PRINCIPLE 4: OVERCOMING INSECURITY AND REJECTION

slander other people. But Peter says that if we don't act as a little child, but go further below and act like a fully-dependent baby, who depends alone on its mother for survival, we will grow in salvation, which is healing, deliverance, and wholeness of the person we are called to be. Then we will grow to fullness in authority and grace that God wants us to walk in.

In the end of Jesus' rebuke to James and John regarding this matter, Jesus said that He did not come to destroy men's lives, but to save them. The scriptures about the Samaritan woman's incident end up in about the same place—they are about growing in respect to salvation or saving our souls. Saving does not mean just salvation from hell and making heaven our home, it means wholeness and deliverance; both physically and mentally. When we decide to put aside feelings of rejection and insecurity that lead us to malicious behavior toward others, it puts us in a place where our souls can be delivered from the hurts that come from rejection, leading us to wholeness and salvation. It doesn't just stop there: our actions will also bring the presence and power of God in our lives, to be seen by all, including the ones who rejected us, leading them to truth.

# PRINCIPLE 5: DIVISION

It seems inevitable that every time God pours out His Spirit and starts to reveal Himself in a new way to the church, a new denomination springs up. Each of them takes to heart what God has given them, and they highlight their revelation as a core theme of their denomination. We see this from the beginning of organized church history straight through today. Unfortunately, once that happens, each group tends to discount or even persecute the other groups, because "they don't do things the way we do" or "they are not a part of our group."

In Luke 9:49-50, we read that this mentality started with the disciples. These verses are sandwiched between Jesus explaining to the disciples what it means to be the greatest and rebuking James and John for wanting to call down fire from heaven on the Samaritans. These two verses are full of very important spiritual truths. The disciple John came to Jesus after being on the road without Him and said, "**Master, we saw someone casting out demons in your name; and we tried to prevent him because he does not follow along with us." But Jesus said to him, "Do not hinder *him;* for he who is not against you is for you."**

What was John thinking here? Was this man a competitor for the authority in the kingdom? Was this man doing it differently than they were? Was this man part of another group? They felt that because the man was not with the disciples and wasn't doing things the way they did, he couldn't be right. They thought that he had to come under their authority to do it the right way; this person needed to be controlled.

Although nothing is recorded in the Bible, this man must have heard Jesus preach and seen Him cast out demons. Maybe he even heard about the disciples doing the same thing. He must have realized the truths that Jesus was talking about, expressed some faith in them, and intended to be a part of what Jesus was doing.

But Jesus told them not to stop people like that man. He said that they were fighting against the kingdom of darkness and that the man was on the same side as the disciples. John was falling into a trap that has plagued the church since the day it was formed: forming a sectarian group. It is the mentality that believes only their own group that has what it takes to do what God wants done in the kingdom. This is not true!

In the Epistles, we see that Paul dealt with this too. He came to Corinth and found divisions among the Corinthians. They were forming groups; there was an Apollos's group, a Paul's group, a Peter's group, and then there was a Christ's group. Let us think this through: what was so unique about each group that made them think that what they believed was more correct or more perfect?

In Acts 18 we hear about Apollos. Apollos was an eloquent man who was preaching the scriptures and teaching about Jesus and repentance (baptism of John), but he wasn't acquainted with the outpouring of the Spirit and the resurrection of Jesus. It is recorded that Priscilla and Aquila explained to Apollos the way to God more accurately. So when Apollos was at Corinth he may have just preached what he knew there and the Corinthians thought that because he was such an eloquent man, God must be with him. Some may have thought that because Peter was a Jew and one of the original twelve apostles, he was more spiritual and so they should follow *him*. After all, Peter was the one to whom Jesus said that He would give the keys of the kingdom, and Peter was also the one who stood up on the day of Pentecost and gave the first message about the risen Christ. Then there was Paul, the most learned of the Pharisees, who was miraculously converted by a vision of Christ that knocked him of his horse and made him temporarily blind; he was also

## PRINCIPLE 5: DIVISION

the one who received divine revelation about the Gentiles being joint heirs with the Jews. So some were convinced that Paul's way was better.

Each of them believed that Jesus was the Messiah, the Christ, and that His work had to be accepted to be saved and translated into the kingdom of God. I'm not sure if these are the exact differences in each group, but the above thoughts illustrate how quickly we can form into groups and denominations. Once we are part of a group we think that we are more accurate and more perfect, so God will manifest Himself more through us. But guess what? We start arguing about our differences rather than rejoicing in what we have in common. Divisions start to form, and the authority of the kingdom in us is weakened.

I like what Paul wrote in 1 Corinthians 3, where he called them infants and babes in Christ, and carnal, acting like the world and acting like men who are not inhabited by Christ and living in the kingdom of God. He said Apollos and Paul are just servants of God, and although each of them had a part to play in their spiritual growth, it is ultimately God who causes the increase and growth. Paul said they were all fellow workers in the kingdom and that the people were God's field and God's building (1 Cor. 3:9). He alone is to be praised; we are not to follow man, but God. Paul knew that we must all give an account to God regarding what we are called to do; that each of us have a part, and when we all do our part, the body of Christ and the kingdom grows individually and corporately.

What I am trying to get across is that God wants us to have a unified love for Him, and because of that devotion, we will have a unified love for one another. Unity does not happen because we all believe the exact same thing and have the exact same doctrine. We should not think that once everyone comes over to our group and believes the same things that we do, we will have unity. We will have unity when we focus on Jesus and determine to come over to His side, keeping our eyes on Jesus, the author and perfecter of our faith.

I am not advocating that we should compromise the core beliefs of the Christian faith. Gordon Lindsay, the founder of Christ for the Nations Bible School in Dallas, Texas, wrote in one of his books that the "mark of error is when we start emphasizing things that are beyond the basic evangelical truths." I think he was saying that we should focus on the major truths, or major commonalities things of our faith, and not on the minor things that divide us.

Paul writes in Colossian 3:14 to put on love, which is the perfect bond of unity—or literally, the uniting bond of perfection (maturity). Let's define the actions and attitude of love as outlined in 1 Corinthians 13: Love is patient with one another; it is kind, showing mercy toward one another. Mercy keeps people from the unfavorable things that they rightfully deserve. Love is not jealous when another succeeds or has notoriety. Jealousy seems to come into play when our goal is to be noticed and commended by people rather than by God. Love does not look to tear others down, but builds others up. It is not arrogant or bragging; arrogance refuses to listen or show regard for others. Arrogance and bragging are normally evidenced by how much we talk about ourselves and our accomplishments. It also can be seen in our attitude toward others when we don't agree with what they are saying. We can disagree with one another, but still show respect for each other. We can disagree without being disagreeable. Love does not think of doing things for its own benefit but thinks of how it can benefit others. This is what goodness is: doing things for the benefit of others—even at one's own expense. Love is not easily provoked to anger that brings retribution to others; it overlooks wrongs suffered. Love chooses to believe the best of others and bears others' burdens.

In fellowship with God one day, the Lord spoke to me about unity. He said something very profound to me, which I think about often. He said, "Unity in the body of Christ is like oxygen to a fire." You could have the largest raging fire, and if all the oxygen were sucked out of the atmosphere, the fire would immediately go out. Our God is a consuming fire, as described in Hebrews 12:29. In numerous places in the Bible, God appeared as a fire. The reason is because God is love, and His love

## PRINCIPLE 5: DIVISION

is so pure and perfect that it appears as a fire. The fuel to His fire is love. Unlike natural fire that destroys everything around it, God's fire only destroys sin and creates life in all of us.

When this denominational/sectarian spirit takes hold of us, it sucks the presence of God out of the church just like when a fire is deprived of oxygen, the fire goes out. Without the presence of God, we are just playing church and becoming religious. The children of Israel knew that if the presence of God was not going to go with them into the Promised Land, they might as well not go. So they repented, and Moses pleaded their case until God decided to go with them.

I'm not saying that God leaves us or that we lose our salvation, but God pulls back from interacting and fellowshipping with us individually and corporately when this sectarian spirit invades us. He waits for us to repent and change. He doesn't want to leave, but He is a holy God who dwells in perfect unity and love. He is waiting for us to come over to His side and understand His ways. As we humble ourselves and ask for His forgiveness, He is ready to flood us again.

Let me give you an example of this. (I am not saying this is the way it happens all the time, but this is a manifestation of what I am talking about.) In Acts 1 and 2, the Bible shows how the disciples were of one mind, continually devoting themselves to prayer with the women, Mary the mother of Jesus, and Jesus' brothers. They were of one mind, or one passion, for the Lord and were continually seeking God. Our passion for God infuses the atmosphere with a spiritual substance that God wants to inhabit. We could also say that human passion and desire for God is like a divine accelerant for His presence. When the day of Pentecost had come, they were in one accord and in one place—both physically and spiritually. Then a rushing mighty wind came from heaven—it was God's fiery presence coming to dwell in man. Some versions translate it as they saw "tongues" of fire. Flames of fire filled the room, then separated and settled on each person. Each person was filled with the Holy Spirit and became a burning bush of His presence. We know what happened from there; the gospel started. It spread in Jerusalem, Judea, and Samaria, and to the uttermost parts of the earth. That is what I call kingdom authority visiting earth through His people!

Over the years, it has been consistent: when you talk to people, no matter what denomination, sect, or movement they choose for worshipping the Lord, there always seems to be an underlying belief that where and how they worship is the closest to how Jesus would have worshiped or wanted us to worship. It usually comes out in several ways. First, it comes out in doctrine, because they believe their doctrines of faith are the closest to the way Jesus taught it and the closest to what is outlined in the New Testament. Sooner or later, this type of mentality comes out: "If you don't believe the way we do, say it the way we do, or act the way we do, then you're missing God."

I am going to make a statement here—doctrine and our adherence to doctrine is overrated in measuring the extent of our spirituality. Why? Because many times we measure our spirituality by how much of the doctrine we may have memorized and hold on to. It is a way we can measure how spiritual we think we are, and how others can measure our spirituality. The problem is that we can memorize a doctrine or a scripture, but if we don't have a personal revelation of it, and the Holy Spirit has not made it real and living inside of us, then we aren't moving any closer to God. A few questions to ask if you think you might be dealing with this issue are: Has the word been written on your heart? Is there life and power to it? If not, then our so-called spirituality is just empty words with no eternal substance behind it.

Much of the church lives this way, trying to live off of someone else's revelation without having received their own fire and revelation. We cannot live a spiritual life and have a relationship with God on someone else's revelation. In Psalm 103, the Psalmist said that Moses knew the ways of God, and the children of Israel knew His acts. That is one of the reasons why they fell in the wilderness; they rejected the personal voice of God in their lives because they were afraid of Him. They told Moses to hear from God and tell them what God said, and then they would obey it. But they could not do it! Until we hear God for ourselves and interact with Him personally, there will be no power behind the Word to transform us.

The church does the same thing with worship and music. Over the years I have seen so many different ways to conduct worship. Some churches sing hymns with the musicians and singers in the back of the church. Some churches just have an organist in front of the church and sing hymns. Some churches have a music band and singers with more contemporary worship. There's no right way, other than that we are to present ourselves to God as a living sacrifice, which is our spiritual service of worship, and yield our bodies and lives as instruments unto God as our worship. By the way, we don't even need music to do that. Music in the church is a ministry to help with worship, but it is not required. Music makes it easier to worship God—but you can worship God without any music at all.

We can go on about different things in the church, from how we pray, to how we baptize, to how we reach out, to how we may do an altar call, to what we believe about the Holy Spirit. The point I am trying to make is that each group and every denomination has a part. We should be willing to learn from each other and realize that each group has a purpose and distinct part. We may think Jesus is waiting for everyone to come over to the side we are on, but in reality, He is just waiting for all of us to come over to His side. The apostle Paul expounds on this in 1 Corinthians12:18–21:

> But now God has placed the members, each one of them, in the body, just as He desired. If they were all one member, where would the body be? But now there are many members, but one body. And the eye cannot say to the hand, "I have no need of you"; or again the head to the feet, "I have no need of you."

There have been so many movements and outpourings of the Holy Spirit throughout church history, and each of them highlight certain things. I believe these are things that God chose to bring to the church for that time period. There are more movements—some larger than others, and more than I could or want to mention in this book—but each of them was a foundation stone in the building of the church. On the day of Pentecost there was the outpouring of the Holy Spirit upon the Jews, signifying that God no longer lives in earthen temples, but inside of us—His people; we have been redeemed and forgiven, and are now the temple of God. A few years later, God brought Paul along to the understanding that this gift of the Holy Spirit and redemption was not just for the Jews, but that the Gentiles (or the rest of the world) were co-heirs of this gift and redemption through faith and could receive the same blessing. Paul also brought the revelation of what happened at the cross—the great exchange—where God took our sin for His righteousness and we received His righteousness for our sin. We received our substitute in Jesus, and then we identified with Jesus by receiving Him, after which God considered us the same as Him. Just as Jesus was crucified, died, buried, quickened, made alive, raised, and seated with God the Father in heavenly places through the work of God, so are we when we express faith in Jesus and receive Him into our lives as our personal Lord and Savior.

Each of these things caused a problem to the established religious order. The Jews persecuted the Jewish Christians, and the Jews and Jewish Christians persecuted the *Gentile* Christians. That pattern has not seemed to change over the years.

Martin Luther, Jan Hus, John Wycliffe, and Huldrich Zwingli brought reformation and revelation to the church regarding principles such as "the just shall live by faith," and the thought that a personal relationship with God should not be controlled by a religious body, along with the revelation that the Word of God (the Bible) should be available to the common man and that God could reveal Himself personally to everyone. Each of them was persecuted, and many of them were martyred for their faith and for the call that God put on their lives. The "current establishment" tried to shut them down because their new wisdom bucked against the excepted norm of faith of their time.

## PRINCIPLE 5: DIVISION

There were so many reformers in the Protestant church, and their teachings spawned many moves of God that turned into many of our modern-day denominations. Among them were the likes of John Calvin, John Knox, Jonathan Edwards, John Fox, Charles Whitfield, and John Wesley (to mention a few). Each time, God would pour out His Spirit on what they were doing, and the previous establishment would always persecute them and try to inhibit the move of God. That is what that "religious denominational spirit" will do to all of us if we don't learn to flow with what God is doing.

John Wesley, along with his brother Charles, founded the Methodists. They brought a new understanding of the work of the Holy Spirit, which they called an additional work of grace. We have come to know this as the baptism of the Holy Spirit. People would fall out under the power of the Holy Spirit as Wesley preached. The Methodists were persecuted at that time for what they believed.

In the mid-1800s during the Second Great Awakening, Charles Finney started to give (what we now call) an altar call at his meetings. He would have people come forward to receive Jesus as their Lord. Finney believed that the doctrines of Calvinism were being taken too far without stressing the personal responsibility of the people to receive and seek out Christ for themselves.

Because this had not been experienced before, Finney was persecuted for and criticized for it. Today, altar calls are often done and accepted in modern churches.

In the early 1900s, Charles Parham and William Seymour taught about the baptism of the Holy Spirit with the manifestation of different tongues. They would "tarry for the Holy Spirit," just like Jesus told His disciples to do before the Day of Pentecost—meaning they would pray and wait for the baptism of the Holy Spirit with the manifestation of speaking in tongues. Then one night, several people received the Holy Spirit and spoke in tongues. William Seymour, who was an uneducated, one-eyed black man, did not receive the Holy Spirit with the manifestation of speaking in tongues at that time. He went out to California to preach about this and started meetings at a house that he was invited to. The Holy Spirit fell, and people were baptized in the Holy Spirit. So many people came to the meeting that they had to move it to a barn on Azusa Street. In those meetings, Seymour was baptized in the Holy Spirit, along with scores of other people. Seymour use to preach with a wooden box over his head; I guess he did this because he did not want people looking to him or at him, but rather at God, because the manifestations of the power of God was so strong with the baptism of the Holy Spirit and the other gifts of the Spirit.

Thousands of people came and visited the Azusa Street meetings, and many men and women were so captivated by what happened there that many received calls to the ministry and were sent out around the world. Numerous churches and denominations sprang up through that move of God. Many of those are still with us today, probably the largest of them being the Assemblies of God. They were persecuted constantly, criticized as being "Holy Rollers" and were mocked in many other ways by the established churches, which were also birthed from previous moves of God that highlighted different things in their day. However, they could not see the move of God in the present movement. They criticized the things that didn't make sense to them. Because of their critical spirit, they did not partake in the blessings that were being poured out.

Several years later, a minister named Kenneth Hagin found in his meetings that people could receive the baptism of the Holy Spirit by the laying on of hands, and that people did not need to tarry for the Holy Spirit, as was taught in the early Pentecostal movement that started at Azusa Street. Hagin preached that if you ask Father God, He will give the Holy Spirit to you, and that people could receive it by the laying on of hands. He would take the listeners through the book of Acts, emphasizing that those Bible-time believers would receive the baptism of the Holy Spirit when hands were laid on them. Or he taught that you could receive the baptism of the Holy Spirit just by asking and believing in faith. In the book of Acts, there are five main instances of the Holy Spirit descending and people being filled in the Spirit and speaking in

## PRINCIPLE 5: DIVISION

various tongues. Acts 2 recounts the Day of Pentecost, when the Holy Spirit was poured out on the Jews in Jerusalem. In Acts 8, we read that when Philip went down to Samaria and preached to the people, Peter and John laid hands on the people to receive the Holy Spirit. In Acts 9, we read that Saul was filled with the Holy Spirit after Ananias laid hands on Him. In Acts 10, we read that as Peter preached to the Gentiles at Cornelius' house, the Holy Spirit fell on them and they begin speaking in other tongues. Lastly, in Acts 19, we read that when Paul came to Ephesus and laid hands on some of the disciples, and they were filled with the Holy Spirit and spoke in tongues and prophesied.

The point I am making is that when it comes to speaking in tongues, at first it was thought that we had to "tarry" because that's what Jesus told the disciples; but we didn't realize that it was a transitional time then, and that once the Holy Spirit was poured out on the day of Pentecost, any believer could receive the Holy Spirit by asking and believing. The church came to a deeper understanding of how to receive the baptism of the Holy Spirit *as time went on*.

This type of progression in revelation has advanced since the inception of the church, especially over the last 150 years. We need to realize that just because we have hold of something God is doing today, does not mean He will add to it tomorrow. Too often we think that once God is doing something with our group, church, or movement, that is the only way He does it! Then when God does something differently in another group, we criticize it before we even understand it. We need to be open-minded, but not so open-minded that our brains fall out, or so closed-minded that if the Holy Spirit where to show up and walk down the isle of our church with an outfit on that says "Holy Spirit," we would not throw Him out for being out of order in the middle of our service.

I remember several years ago, sitting in an elder's meeting in a very large church that I was a part of. God had wonderfully raised this church up. It grew to about 1,500 people and was doing well. We were excited about what God was doing and were believing for God to move in our midst. I asked the other elders in that meeting, "What makes us so sure that when the next move of God comes, we will not miss it and do the same thing other groups have done?" I looked at everyone and was waiting for a response. No one responded, and then the senior pastor went on to change the subject. The reality was that we were falling into the same pattern as other movements that grew up with the power of God. I can remember a few times when the Holy Spirit showed up in a different form and fashion than we were used to. We didn't flow with it—we may have missed the blessing God wanted to impart to us.

This closed-minded thinking is just another form of the religious sectarian spirit that tries to divide us rather than unite us. We need to be discerning; not so quick to jump on every new thing that comes down the pike, but not so slow that we cannot see the fruit and the power of God on something new.

I'm not talking about trying to build things that are not scriptural, but just because we haven't noticed it in the scriptures yet, does not mean it's not there. As God reveals something new, we will be able to see it woven throughout the Bible. We might find some reference to it in the books of the Law, in the books of Wisdom Literature, in the books of the Major and/or Minor Prophets, or somewhere taught in the Gospels, and then reinforced in the Epistles.

We need to be diligent to never allow this sectarian religious spirit to creep up on us. It's so easy to get comfortable in what we have and know; we miss out on the "more" that we can have with God. The disciples were stopping someone from casting out a demon just because that person was not a part of their group. They were more concerned about people being a part of their group than about a person being blessed and delivered from the evil spirit that was binding him or her. Before we start to criticize someone for doing something that is different than the way our denomination or group does, we need to ask ourselves why we are criticizing them. What are our motives in being critical? What are all the facts around what is going on? What fruit is coming out of it? Is there a humility and grace upon what is going on? Is God getting glory? Once we get those answers, then it would be better for us to stop, seek the face of God, and pray to find out from God what He thinks about it! If we don't do this, too often we will fall into a trap of criticizing something God is in.

# PRINCIPLE 6: NEW WINE AND NEW WINE SKINS

I want to add to the previous chapter and build on it with something that Jesus said in the Gospels. One day while I was in prayer I heard the Holy Spirit speak to me. He said, "I want new wine skins for new wine, because I want to **preserve the flavor of both the old and the new wine**." I thought this was very interesting, because I was always one who wanted to be at the forefront of what I saw God doing, and to a degree, I would frown on older religious orders.

As I started to think about this, my attention was brought to the parable that Jesus taught on this subject which can be found in three of the four Gospels: Luke 5:36-39, Matthew 9:15-17, and Mark 2:18-22. I would like to use Matthew's rendition of this parable:

> Then the disciples of John came to Him, asking, "Why do we and the Pharisees fast, but your disciples do not fast?" And Jesus said to them, "The attendants of the bridegroom cannot mourn as long as the bridegroom is with them, can they? But the days will come when the bridegroom is taken away from them, and then they will fast. "But no one puts a patch of unshrunk cloth on an old garment; for the patch pulls away from the garment, and a worse tear results. "**Nor do people put new wine into old wineskins; otherwise the wineskins burst, and the wine pours out and the wineskins are ruined; but**

**they put new wine into fresh wineskins, and both are preserved**" (Matthew 9:14-17).

Jesus was being questioned by John's disciples as to why He did not fast like them and the Pharisees (religious leaders of the day). Fasting was a practice that was well-known in the law and in the Jewish tradition. What was the underlying message in this question? The underlying message was that they always fasted, and in order to be spiritual and more like God, and to do His will, the disciples had to do the same thing. I'm not sure if this question was more accusative or perplexing. But the question points to the same thing: if you don't do it the way it has always been done and accepted, there must be something wrong with you and your practices.

Jesus was letting them know that there is a time and a season for all things, but this was not the time for them to fast. Jesus told them to stop looking through religious eyes and look through spiritual eyes instead. He taught them through parables so they could understand this.

Wineskins were used to ferment wine, and as the wine would ferment, the skin would expand. As I was meditating on this, I got the distinct impression that if the old wineskins could expand and ferment the new wine, because wine had already been in that wineskin, the old skin would have taken on the flavor of the old wine, and the flavor of the new wine would mingle with the flavor of the old. The result, the distinctiveness of the new wine could not be experienced, and its value would be diminished or entirely lost. The unique flavors of both the old and the new wine cannot be distinguished. Jesus specifically said that we are not to put new wine in old wineskins so the flavor of both could be preserved.

The same grapevines produce grapes every year, but based on many environmental factors, the flavor of the wine produced from each group may vary. Some crops might produce a more flavorful wine, but each crop has its own distinction and is useful for consumption.

## PRINCIPLE 6: NEW WINE AND NEW WINE SKINS

This parable is an illustration about not falling into that sectarian or denominational spirit. We can always learn something and taste something from a previous generation. This problem has continually followed the church. It can be found in the book of Acts. Jesus said that the gospel will be preached in Jerusalem, Judea, and Samaria, and to the uttermost parts of the earth.

The book of Acts begins with the narrative of the outpouring of the Holy Spirit in Jerusalem on the day of Pentecost. This was an outpouring upon the Jews. Much of the first seven chapters of the book of Acts are about what God was doing in Jerusalem, In Acts 6:7 (my paraphrase), "Then the word of God spread, and the number of the disciples multiplied greatly in Jerusalem, and a great many of the priests were obedient to the faith." Then in chapter 7, we read about Stephen and his testimony and martyrdom. His testimony was to the Jews, and the Jews were the ones who stoned him. In chapter 8, we read that the word was preached in Samaria, and the outpouring of the Holy Spirit happened there. But because the Samaritans were still of Jewish blood, it was still about the Holy Spirit being poured on the Jewish people.

I call this the first outpouring of the Holy Spirit in the New Testament, or the first wave of the Holy Spirit, or the first harvest of wine taking place. The revelation and the outpouring were that Jesus was the Christ and Savior, and that God no longer dwelt in earthen temples, but dwells in man. God validated this outpouring with signs and wonders. In chapter 9 we read that Saul was converted. In chapter 10 we read about the second outpouring of the Holy Spirit; which starts with the next harvest of wine. The Gentiles were also included with this outpouring. Cornelius sends for Peter after his vision. Peter also had a vision and comes to preach Jesus as the Christ. The Holy Spirit was poured out so heavily that as he was preaching, they were filled with the Holy Spirit and they spoke in tongues.

This really upset the theology of the Jews and the Jewish Christians. Peter comes back to Jerusalem in Acts 11. The apostles heard what had happened, and those of the circumcision contended with Peter, meaning they were angry and wanted to separate themselves from Peter because he entered the house of the Gentiles and preached the gospel. Peter told them what happened supernaturally, and for a time they all rejoiced and were happy that God poured His Spirit out on the Gentiles.

Peter was one of the main figures God used in the first outpouring and was a transitional figure in the second outpouring. But Paul was going to be the main figure to carry the torch for the new "revelation," or new "wine," that was being preached in the church. In Acts 13 we read that Paul and Barnabas set out on their first missionary journey. Paul first went to the Jews. Because they didn't accept him, he went to the Gentiles. The Gentiles would accept the gospel and then the Jews would stir up some strife, just to create a problem for Paul.

After Paul's first missionary journey, he and Barnabas came back to Jerusalem. The council took them up to question them of their preaching to the Gentiles. Paul confirmed that it was the call and plan of God. But as time went on, more and more untrue stores were coming out of Paul's ministry and the many priests who came to the faith were gaining more and more control. They could not see that both the old and the new wine were there for a purpose. They were not mutually exclusive. In the end, Paul was beaten and imprisoned for preaching the gospel to the Gentiles. More than likely, some of these people were those who experienced the outpouring of the Holy Spirit on the day of Pentecost not too many days before this happened.

# PRINCIPLE 8: AMBITION—IS IT FROM HEAVEN OR EARTH?

In an earlier chapter, we talked about the disciples discussing as to who the greatest among them was. We spent three chapters going over each situation. We introduced the occurrence of Peter rebuking Jesus for telling them that He was going to the cross and was going to die and rise again in three days. Peter said to Jesus, "May this never be." Jesus rebuked Peter for his selfish ambitions. Peter was not seeking first God's kingdom; instead he was seeking to build his own kingdom first, which he thought was a subset of God's kingdom. I don't think Peter understood what he was doing at the time. But as we discussed earlier, he came into a much deeper revelation of this and wrote about it in his epistle of 1 Peter.

James also wrote about this in his epistle. Let's take some time and discuss this subject. Until God reveals what is in our heart, it is very difficult for us to understand the evils of selfish ambition and how it invades our heart and affects our judgment and actions. I also want to dissect the difference between basic ambition and selfish ambition. We all have a desire to succeed and accomplish something noteworthy in our lives, both from a secular and spiritual point of view, but how we go about it can really reveal our true spirituality.

If you think about it, Jesus had ambition—it was a deep passion to fulfill the will of the Father, go to the cross, and redeem man. The scriptures tell us that He set His face like flint to go to Jerusalem, so much that the Samaritans got mad at Him when He was going to pass through Samaria to go to Jerusalem and told them that He was not going to stop there. Paul also had a determined ambition and passion for the kingdom; he had to, in order to endure all he did in all his missionary trips, imprisonments, and persecutions. But we need to understand that just because we want to do something for the kingdom of God, it doesn't mean we will automatically do it the way God wants us to. We can understand or perceive the plans of God, but we might pursue His plans in our own way because our ultimate purpose is not always aligned with God's.

There is something in each of us that affects us. Some call it the unrenewed nature, or the ego, or the flesh. John talks about it in 1 John 2:15-16:

> Do not **love** the world nor the things in the world. If anyone **loves** the world, the **love** of the Father is not in him. For all that is in the world, the lust of the flesh and the lust of the eyes and the boastful pride of life, is not from the Father, but is from the world.

John calls it the lust of the flesh, which is the desire of the flesh to exalt itself. This happens when we look at the accomplishments we have and attribute them more to ourselves rather than God. The lust of the eyes desires to accumulate to ourselves things to our own glory, and the pride of life says, "Look at me and what I have accomplished."

Paul talks about this in his letter to the Ephesians. In chapter 2 he says that there is a spirit in this fallen world system that plays on our weakness of the flesh and tries to influence us to walk and act in ways that feed our ego and pride. When this happens, we will do things for our own benefit at the expense of others. Our success and status will motivate how we treat others; we will use others in our pursuits, and when people don't benefit our pursuits we disregard them—and even malign them.

## PRINCIPLE 8: AMBITION—IS IT FROM HEAVEN OR EARTH?

One morning while I was in prayer, the Lord asked me a very profound question. He asked, "Why am I good?" As I pondered how to answer, I thought it would be better for me to say nothing and instead just ask the Lord to tell me something, because I was sure that there was more to the answer than what I knew. The Lord said to me, "I am good because everything I do is for the benefit of others, even when it is at My own expense." What an amazing statement! As I thought about this, I realized that the ultimate example of this was the sacrifice the Son made on the cross. God the Father sent the Son; Jesus sacrificed the glory of sitting at the right hand of the Father and became man, then He sacrificed the exaltation of man and went to the cross to redeem mankind.

Let's go back to Matthew chapter 16 where Peter rebuked Jesus for telling the disciples that he was going to be mistreated at the hands of the religious leaders, die, and then rise again on the third day. Was Peter's motivation for the benefit of others, or was his motivation primarily for his own benefit and possible future position in the kingdom? I believe the answer was the latter; that is why Jesus rebuked him. On the surface, what Peter said was admirable because he was protecting Jesus; but underneath, it was evil.

Unless we see and hear the way God does, we will never truly discern what is good and evil. The writer of Hebrews talks about this in chapter 5. He says,

> Solid food is for the mature because they have had their spiritual senses deeply exercised, so they can discern the difference between good and evil (Hebrews 5:14).

It takes continual practice and interaction with the Living God, learning and understanding His ways, studying His Word, and communing with the Holy Spirit to discern good and evil. This doesn't come overnight. Understanding His ways doesn't mean that we have learned a doctrine or memorized a scripture; it means we have eaten the Word and digested it, and the Word has become flesh inside of us and has become a part of us. We then carry the Living Word, known and read by all men around us. This process usually results in stripping away all human pride and exposing it for its wretchedness before God rebuilds us in a union with Him in will and purpose.

This is such an important truth because this is what Adam and Eve failed at. They did not discern that the motives of the serpent and their own were evil. They ate of the Tree of Knowledge of Good and Evil. It is also the basis of what all believers will be judged for at the judgment seat of Christ, as spoken about in the New Testament. The judgment seat of Christ is a place of judgment for believers, for the works that they have done in the body; it is a place where rewards will be given, and things will be exposed for their true motives and intentions. In 2 Corinthians 5:10, we read that we will be rewarded for things done in the body whether good or bad (evil).

James says this so profoundly in his epistle:

> If you are wise and understand God's ways, prove it by living an honorable life, doing good works with the humility that comes from wisdom. But if you are bitterly jealous and there is selfish ambition in your heart, don't cover up the truth with boasting and lying. For jealousy and selfishness is not God's kind of wisdom. Such things are earthly, unspiritual, and demonic. For wherever there is jealousy and selfish ambition, there you will find disorder and evil of every kind.
>
> But the wisdom from above is first of all pure. It is also peace **loving**, gentle at all times, and willing to yield to others. It is full of mercy and good deeds. It shows no favoritism and is always sincere. And those who are peacemakers will plant seeds of peace and reap a harvest of righteousness (James 3:13-18 NLT).

I like that James starts off by noting how God accomplishes things with wisdom and understanding, and that the way He goes about doing things

## PRINCIPLE 8: AMBITION—IS IT FROM HEAVEN OR EARTH?

is much different than man. The prophet Isaiah said that as high as the heavens are above the earth, so are God's ways above our ways. That is why God is so holy; all that He does transcends measurement. If we don't take note of that, our ways will fall short of what God wants to do in and through us. Psalm 103 says that Moses knew the ways of God and the children of Israel new the acts of God. That's one of the reasons why the children of Israel fell in the wilderness: they rejected God talking to them directly and told Moses, "You hear God and we will do what you say." The problem is that we cannot live our spiritual life based on another person's revelation. We need to get our own revelation and establish our own intimacy with God, then the Word will become flesh in us and will live in us so we can know and understand how to walk in the ways of God.

The ways of God are motivated by good, which means our motives for doing things are for the betterment of others, even when what we are trying to do will result in things that may not be to our benefit. God's ways are always motivated by humility, which is a position of complete dependence on the God who loves, accepts, and lives in truth. This truth is so pure that even after being examined under the purest light for dissection, it is deemed righteous.

James also describes it as peace-loving. One day the Lord gave me a definition of His peace. He said, "Peace is the prosperity of your harmonious relationship with God." It is the result of being in union and harmony with God and His ways. So those who have peace will always seek to stay in harmony with God. Jesus said, "Blessed are the peacemakers, for they will be called the sons of God." All peace starts with God. The only way we will have peace without division is when we seek to be in harmony with God. Too often, splits and division come because we get into a position to choose sides over some issue, forcing us to go to one side or the other. If we all would choose to go over to God's side, then peace and harmony would take care of itself.

God's wisdom is gentle; another word for that is meek. Let me give you give another "God definition." *Meekness* is "power under control, submitted to the will of God." People who are meek use their power and authority to help and do well. They will refrain from using their authority to willingly hurt others, even if they feel threatened. Too often, authorities abuse their power and destroy and tear down people who may threaten their authority, or abuse their authority to manipulate people to do things they don't want to do. Jesus was the epitome of meekness: all His power was always submitted to the will of God. When He could have sent His angels to fight for Him while He was being taken to the cross, He did not. He knew that the will of God was the cross. Meekness will always yield to others and will not try to promote self in any situation that could cause strife. Meekness will always seek the will, judgment, and dominion of God. That is why the meek will inherit the earth. Meekness trusts in the sovereign will and purposes of God. Meekness will allow the dominion of the kingdom to rule, just as Jesus said, "Blessed are the poor in spirit for theirs is the kingdom of God." The poor in spirit realize that they are utterly bankrupt in their human abilities to bring about the will of God, and know that they need the interaction, wisdom, and power of the one true God living inside them.

Jealousy and selfish ambition will always seek to divide and conquer; and when it does there will be strife and decision and disunity. I want to describe this behavior and take you through a discourse Jesus had on this subject. People who are motivated by these two fleshly forces can be obsessive and vicious in trying to prove that they are right; they want to get a position of advantage rather than having a rational persuasion of the truth. They regard people who disagree with them as enemies who need to be destroyed rather than colleagues who need to be persuaded. They will cover the truth by subtly twisting it in order to give themselves an advantage. They will give you enough of the truth to help their position, but will conveniently leave out the entirety of the truth because it will not be to their advantage. As a result, they are concerned with displaying the truth that will help them to be victorious in the situation—even when their victory comes at the expense of the reputation and hurt of others. They win— and that is all that matters to them. Their arrogance in the situation will not make room for any other

## PRINCIPLE 8: AMBITION—IS IT FROM HEAVEN OR EARTH?

opinion and they would rather point to the shortcomings of the people voicing alternate opinions to discredit them and build their own case. In the end, this spirit will cause strife, dissension, and hurt. This is the root of so many church splits.

I believe Jesus addressed this type of behavior in a discussion that was recorded in Matthew 7. The Lord showed me this through my own actions in the spirit of selfish ambition and jealousy. He revealed how my acts of trying to prove myself right did not accomplish what I intended to do. The reality is that I was right, but I was more concerned with proving my rightness than trying to understand why the person was doing what they were doing and trying to help them see that what they were doing was not in their own best interest. I just wanted to blast them with the truth. We have heard that an open correction is better than concealed love, and we are to speak the truth in love. But I also learned that just because we speak the truth doesn't mean that we have always spoken it in love.

If selfish ambition and/or jealousy is in our heart, we can use the truth to accuse and tear down rather than correct and build up. Paul says that we need to restore others with the spirit of meekness, knowing that but for the grace of God, we could be caught in the same situation. James says here that this ambition, or jealousy-based type of wisdom, is demonic; meaning that it is motivated and inspired by earthly demonic forces. The devil will use a twisted form of the truth to manipulate and control us. This type of spirit motivates us to be more concerned with correction and punishment rather than restoration and growth of the person.

The reason this happens is because the truth is not tempered with mercy. Mercy keeps from us the punishment that we rightfully deserve, and grace gives us the blessings that we don't deserve. That is how God brings us to change: it is the manifestation of His goodness. There are several passages in Proverbs that talk about this. Proverbs 3:3-4 says not to let mercy and truth leave us, that we are to bind them around our neck and have them written on our hearts, and that we will find favor and good understanding in the sight of God and man. Proverbs 16:6 says that by mercy and truth, iniquity is purged: meaning sin and error can be corrected and eliminated from one's life when mercy is the motivation behind the truth.

For years I had heard and taught Hosea 4:6, which says, "My people have been destroyed for lack of knowledge because they have rejected knowledge." But I never read the verses that preceded it. In verse 1 of the same chapter, the prophet tells us what knowledge they need. He says that **because *there is* no truth, nor mercy, nor knowledge of God in the land,** there is no knowledge of God.

Hebrews 4 says that the Word of God is living and active and sharper than any two-edged sword, and that when the truth of the Word comes forth, it judges and discerns the thoughts and true intents of the heart. We all know that being cut with a (spiritual) sword to reach our deepest thoughts and intentions can hurt. But God doesn't leave us there; He assures us that we have a great High Priest who can sympathize with the weakness of the flesh, and if we come to Him, He will lead us to the throne of grace. At the throne of grace is where we receive mercy, forgiveness, and acceptance, which keeps us from what we deserve—judgment. Grace gives us what we don't deserve; it changes us and transforms us into His image, empowering us to walk in His ways and judgments.

So, getting back to the story in Matthew 7:3-5 (NLT):

> "And why worry about a speck in your friend's eye, when you have a log in your own? How can you think of saying to your friend, 'Let me help you get rid of that speck in your eye,' when you can't see past the log in your own eye? Hypocrite! First get rid of the log in your own eye; then you will see well enough to deal with the speck in your friend's eye."

The speck is a little piece of dirt; the log really means a beam—like a supporting beam in a roof. When we are concerned with the speck in

## PRINCIPLE 8: AMBITION—IS IT FROM HEAVEN OR EARTH?

others' eyes, our motivation is not with God's wisdom. In the situation I mentioned earlier, I saw myself correcting this person rather than going to him with a small tip-like instrument to take his "speck" out, I went with a Samurai sword and cut off the whole area of the problem. The reality is that I got rid of the speck, but I flayed the individual so badly that he may never recover from his wounds. In the spirit, I saw my friend so bloodied and hurt from the correction that it would take him months to heal—if he could even heal at all.

The Lord then said to me, "You need to be like a trained surgeon who sees an area of tissue that is infected with a disease and does everything to cut out the infected area and minimize tissue damage to the surrounding areas. This will correct the situation and minimize the time necessary for recovery because the other surrounding good tissues were not hurt during the operation."

A perfect example for this comes to my mind. Not so long ago someone I know had torn the cartilage in their knee and had to have their knee cut open to repair the cartilage. Because the incision had to be large, it would take the patient at least three or four months, if not longer, to heal. But in recent years, we have developed arthroscopic surgery, where a small incision is made, a scope is inserted into the knee, and the cartilage is repaired—leaving the patient with a recovery time of only three to four *weeks*.

If I would have gone in with a gentle and meek spirit and spoken the truth in a way that brought correction and restoration lovingly, the result would have been much more profitable. However, the result I brought about in the flesh just created a wedge in our relationship.

If our motivation is tempered and inspired by God and we walk in His wisdom, we can be wise master surgeons, doing the necessary correction in a way that restoration and healing can happen without fleshly-inspired additional pain and suffering.

Let's look at what James writes about the characteristics of God's wisdom:

> But the wisdom from above is first of all pure. It is also peace **loving**, gentle at all times, and willing to yield to others. It is full of mercy and good deeds. It shows no favoritism and is always sincere. And those who are peacemakers will plant seeds of peace and reap a harvest of righteousness (James 3:17-18 NLT).

Pure wisdom is holy, and when examined by God's perfect light, it is deemed without any ulterior motive. Peace loving means that it is patient and kind—it is not jealous, does not seek its own, it bears, believes and hopes in all things (does this sound familiar?) It is willing to yield to others in meekness. It is full of the right combination of mercy and truth to plant peace and restoration. These ingredients together create a planting of the Lord that will increase and grow and bear fruit for the kingdom.

In James chapter 4 he goes on with the subject to say that if there are division, strife, and arguments among people, they are fueled by evil desires. Again, the source of evil and how God looks at what is evil and what is good are much different than what we perceive. Evil is fueled by self-centered ambition, doing what is primarily for our own benefit; and while doing that, we are less concerned with the benefit of others and more concerned with our own. We get more concerned about our attainment and satisfaction than we are with the overall betterment of other people.

James says that our jealously will drive us to fight and get what we want, and we will devise schemes to kill in order to get them. It sure sounds like how Jesus described the devil! He said that the devil comes to steal, kill, and destroy. He also said that the devil is a liar and was a liar from the beginning, and that there is no truth in him. Although people don't usually physically kill people all the time, John explains in his writing that if we hate our brother we walk in darkness, and that in hating, we cause another to stumble in a way that causes hurt and loss to them. John points to Cain and how he killed his brother Abel because of his jealousy. He goes on to say that when we hate, we are the same as a

## PRINCIPLE 8: AMBITION—IS IT FROM HEAVEN OR EARTH?

murderer, but a true sign of being led by God and walking in the light is our love for the brethren.

We can walk this fault out in many ways without physically killing our brother or sister. We can expose their faults to discredit them or we can malign and speak evil of them, so they get a wrong reputation. I can remember situations in church leadership where the senior leader had an issue with someone because they were posed to be a challenge to them. This challenge could have been motivated because of jealousy regarding that person's spiritual gifts, or because that person was trying to correct the senior leader for a wrong that they had done. We could go on to discuss many ways this could happen, but we won't at this point. In response to the challenge, the leader, in order to discredit them, would infuse bad seeds in other people with his thoughts about the person's shortcoming or faults until it would get around the church, with the intent that this would stop the challenging person and discredit anything they said. But often this would just add fuel to the fire by causing a bigger rift, which in the end leads to broken relationships and people leaving an assembly.

We can easily be caught in these situations before we know it. We become vessels of gossip for the leadership, thinking we are doing the senior leader a favor and getting in his good graces. I can honestly admit that there have been times where I have fallen into this trap. I was more concerned with my calling and position than I was with the truth and the call on my life to love people. It exposed me in ways that forever has branded itself on my mind. The result was the death of relationships, the death of fellowship, and a wedge between me and God— and it also decreased the true authority of the kingdom working through me. In situations like this we sacrifice someone, and whether we know it or not, the part that they contribute is not there to edify and increase the body.

James refers to all of this as "friendship with the world," meaning that you have an affection and agreement with how the world may do things. I have seen these types of things happen in the business world so often, where people try to discredit and hurt another to gain a position or advantage over someone else. People in the business world tend to say, "this is just business," which is just an excuse to hide behind evil motives and selfish gain, demonstrated in lying, cheating, and manipulating the truth for one's own benefit at the expense of others. It is not "just business," it is selfish manipulation.

These types of behaviors do not help the secular or non-secular world. They will not bear fruit for the kingdom, and they will not allow us to walk in the true authority of the kingdom. The meekness and humility of the Lamb will result in us individually, and in the church, globally walking in the true authority of the Lion, which will in turn affect the world and the institutions around us in ways that only God could accomplish.

# PART 4: MASTER BUILDER PRINCIPLES 8-9—HUMILITY AND THE CROSS

# PRINCIPLE 8: HUMILITY, PART 1

### *"The virtue of virtues"*

We've talked about humility a few times in previous chapters, but now we are going to camp on it for a while.

Humility is the divine substance of God that empowers and guides us down the paths of God's ways, judgments, and actions. Humility is a habitation where God is everything and we are nothing. It's a place of dependence upon God that comes from the understanding of the utter weakness and powerlessness of man to attain the perfection of God on his own. Humility is how we accept the truth and do not run from it; we embrace it no matter how exposing and hurtful it may be. Humility doesn't come because we want it or think it's spiritual. It comes from interacting with God and seeing things from His perspective and realizing how He reacts to things. When we are exposed to the true nature of God we are awed by His beauty and perfection. We are drawn, and in the drawing we get exposed to it and it transforms us into what He is like.

In chapter 4 of his epistle, the apostle James says that God gives grace to the humble and opposes the proud. When he says that God opposes the proud, it means that God stands resolutely against it. Pride will try to exalt self and the ways of man. In the end, bringing acknowledgment to man rather than to God. Pride can be used to explain every human error and weakness. Pride will say, "I know better than God; I can show God how to do it." Pride will tell God, "Look, if I do this, it will make me better, even though You said it would not."

> You adulterers! Don't you realize that friendship with the world makes you an enemy of God? I say it again: If you want to be a friend of the world, you make yourself an enemy of God. Do you think the Scriptures have no meaning? They say that God is passionate that the spirit he has placed within us should be faithful to him (James 4:4-5 NLT).

Let me give you an example of what friendship with the world looks like. The word friendship here is the Greek word *philia*, derived from the word *philos*, which is where the root of the name of the city "Philadelphia" comes from, the city of brotherly love. It refers to a deep friendship and familiarity that influences you. This is what Jesus was trying to get the apostles to understand as He was training them. He was teaching them that one cannot build God's kingdom on worldly principles of leadership. Sometimes when we think about friendship with the world we think about partaking in worldly things like excessive drinking, wild partying, and illicit sexual behavior, which can all be classified as worldly or as friendship with the world. James was talking about something much different: he was talking to the church that was filled with envy, strife, and selfish ambition.

The apostles' constant argument about who was the greatest was all fueled by selfish ambition. They were trying to manipulate the situation for their own personal advantage and gain. This is worldly behavior, and God stands against it. In Jesus' conversations that He had with the apostles while they were arguing about being the greatest or who had the highest position of authority under Jesus, He gave them an explanation of how the kingdom will operate. Jesus told them (in Luke 24:24-32) that they were not to exercise and rule in the same way the worldly leadership rules. They should not boast and throw their weight around as a leader. He told them not to draw attention to who they are and the authority they have, but rather to act as a servant of one another. If we

## PRINCIPLE 8: HUMILITY, PART 1

have authority over someone and if we want them to really recognize it, we need to become a servant to them. Jesus said, "I have come to serve you as a leader, so do the same."

I have come to realize that man is ignorant of the depths of pride that is present in him. I remember years ago, I was introduced to a little yellow book that is about ninety pages long called *Humility* by Andrew Murray. The book looked harmless, but as I read it I felt God exposing every area where pride was residing inside me—from top to bottom. I got a holy makeover, but I also received great grace for transformation and change. I have re-read that book more times than I can count. But each time I read it brings another transformation in me; it is not always pleasant, but it is very fruitful. At the back of the book is a prayer in which Andrew Murray challenges us to pray for an extended period of time. It goes something like this: "Lord, please reveal in me all levels of pride, whether it be of myself or evil spirits, and root them out of my life." The first time I read the prayer, I thought that it was a "nice" prayer, so I started praying it. I eventually found that there was nothing nice about it: I had just invited a Holy God to expose me! It started out as two of the most painfully-transparent weeks of my young Christian life. During those two weeks, it seemed like everyone around me felt that it was their duty to tell me what was wrong with me and how prideful I was. Rather than argue or point out their shortfalls, I just had to just say, "Thank you. May I have some more." After two weeks, I asked the Lord to please stop. He seemed to have ignored that prayer and has continued to work these truths in me ever since.

There is a process we all go through just like the apostles did. So let me walk you through Peter's progression on this, starting in the Gospels and ending in his epistles.

Peter started seeing all the things Jesus did and comes to the realization that Jesus is the Messiah who all of Israel has been waiting for; Jesus is the one Moses and all the prophets talked about and Jesus is the one who will set up God's kingdom. Peter hears Jesus constantly talk about the kingdom. Then Peter looks around him and sees that he is one of twelve men chosen by Jesus to help carry out God's plans.

Jesus then asks the disciples, "Who do people say I am?" (See Matthew 16:13 and Luke 9:18.) They answered Him with what they had heard others say, at which point He posed the question directly to them. Peter stepped forth and said boldly, "You are the Christ, the Son of the living God." Jesus told Peter that he had gotten a divine revelation from the Father in heaven. This revelation was about a rock, the foundation upon which He would build His church, the assembly of those who believe in Jesus.

I want to point out something very important before I go further in this story. Jesus said He was going to build His church on revelation—and not on doctrine. Revelation imparts the substance of God and brings us to a place of personal experience of the knowledge of God. Revelation is what brings grace and authority to us in the kingdom. Doctrine, which is a statement of belief, doesn't do anything for us if the truth and substance of the doctrine is not made real to each of us personally. Without personal revelation, there is no power or authority behind doctrine. Too many people in the church place their trust in doctrine which the church has no personal revelation about. Personal revelation brings an intimate understanding. We need to experience and then trust in the revelation that comes from the Holy Spirit.

Back to the story: Jesus tells Peter that He will give the disciples the keys of the kingdom of heaven, so whatever they bind on earth would be bound in heaven, and whatever they loose on earth would be loosed in heaven. This was a direct reference to having authority. Just like earthly kings had the authority to rule, bind, and loose, the disciples would have that authority in God's kingdom. The keys signify that those who hold the keys have been given the authority to release the power of the kingdom of heaven, and these keys can release more power than all the authority that the gates of hell could ever put together.

## PRINCIPLE 8: HUMILITY, PART 1

These keys were not just given to Peter, they were given to the church (the assembly of believers). Later on, Jesus talks to all the disciples about the power of binding and loosing (Matthew 18:20). We understand today that this authority has been transferred from the Father to the Son, and the Son has allowed us to be partakers of it because we are all joint heirs with Jesus.

As I reviewed the Gospels, I came to the realization that all those arguments about who would be the greatest in the kingdom started after Jesus told them about the keys of the kingdom being given to them. Jesus had spoken something very powerful. The disciples put a worldly interpretation on what Jesus said, which was distorted in their minds because it was fueled by their own selfish ambition and desire for power, even though they might not have even understood what they were doing.

It started right away with Peter. Just after this big commendation in Matthew 16, Jesus started to tell them about His upcoming death and sacrifice. The disciples had to be thinking, "This doesn't compute. We just heard about the keys to the kingdom, authority, leadership, rulership, and Jesus being the head ruler and bringing about this kingdom and how He will be giving us authority, and now He says that He's going to die? How can He create a kingdom and rule in it and die?" Peter, being emboldened, spoke what everyone was thinking. He took Jesus aside, rebuked Him, and basically told Jesus, "This can't happen!" Jesus, knowing the frailties and motives of men, immediately rebuked Peter saying, "Get behind me, Satan!" He told Peter the equivalent of, "You are thinking like Satan because you are acting on your own selfish ambitions. You need to forget yourself and lose sight of your own promotion and self-interest, and come to a place of submission to God!" Then Jesus gave an analogy of the cross that He was going to bear. They must have had some knowledge of what Jesus meant because crucifixion was a common practice by the Romans, but they may not have had a real understanding until Jesus fulfilled His work on the cross. Many years later, the Apostle Paul wrote about the spiritual work that happened from the cross to the throne.

I can imagine Peter just standing there as Jesus walked away, totally flabbergasted, undone, embarrassed, and confused. He must have been thinking, "I was just trying to fulfill my role as a ruler in Your upcoming kingdom and trying to protect You from harm. Didn't You just give me the keys of the kingdom? Am I not a key player in Your kingdom? How can You call me Satan and tell me I am filled with selfishness?"

God takes us all through a process of cleansing, refining, and stripping us of things. Let's review how this happened to Peter, as an example. As time progressed, the disciples kept arguing about who was the greatest. We will not run through all the scenarios again. Jesus knew His time was short and He was having His last supper with His disciples. They were reclining at the table, and Jesus was talking about His betrayal, and promised them that they would sit at His table in the kingdom, judging the twelve tribes of Israel (see Luke 22:30).

Jesus told Peter that Satan wanted to sift him like wheat, meaning he would do everything to rattle his cage to get him to question his faith in Jesus and keep him from fulfilling his purpose. Jesus told us that Satan will come to steal, kill, and destroy. How does he do this? He primarily wants to steal our relationship with God by getting us to question God's plan and love for us. In doing that he will separate us from the life of God. Killing, to the devil, is to separate us from the One who gives life. Killing is the process of taking the life out of something. The devil tries to strangle us with doubt, fear, guilt, and shame. If we choose to believe his lies, they suck the life of God out of us. They—and he—can destroy us.

Jesus had faith in Peter. Knowing that, Jesus prayed for him with confidence that after he fell, Peter would return to the Lord and be able to encourage and strengthen his brethren.

Peter boasted that he would sacrifice himself unto prison and even unto death for Jesus' sake. We are so often unaware of our frailties, and if we stand on our own power, we will always fall short of what we think we can do. After Peter's bold assertion, Jesus told him that he would deny

## PRINCIPLE 8: HUMILITY, PART 1

Him three times. Peter must have been flabbergasted and perplexed again, probably saying to himself, "No way, Jesus! I will never do this!" At the same time Peter had to know that Jesus is Lord and not prone to being wrong.

When Jesus was taken into custody by the religious leaders, Luke records that Peter struck a man's ear with his sword and cut it off. Jesus stopped him and told him, "no more of this." He then healed the guard and told Peter, "That is not how we are going to fight." Jesus knew that earthy fighting would just put a wrench in the attack plan of heaven. Peter showed courage and followed the guards who took Jesus. He stood outside the courtyard with other people as the authorities questioned Jesus.

Peter must not have been too far away from the house of the high priest where Jesus was brought. He must have been in sight of what was going on with Jesus. According to Luke, within an hour Peter was asked by three different people if he was part of the group that was with Jesus. He denied it all three times. He may have thought that they suspected that he was trying to get information about where Jesus was so later he could go and find a way to rescue Jesus. So Peter could have been denying being a part of Jesus' group. Peter obviously wasn't sensitive to what Jesus had just prophesied a few minutes prior. Then the rooster crowed. The sound of that rooster must have been like a modern-day air horn in his ears. The reality of what Jesus said had come to pass. He just realized it. To make matters worse, right at that moment Jesus must have looked through an opening in the house and caught Peter's eye in the courtyard.

Peter must have said to himself, "I thought I would never do that! How did that just happen?" I imagine that his thoughts and emotions must have come in like a rushing river of condemnation. I can hear the accuser saying, "Didn't you say you would not deny him, and yet you did! You're worthless, you're not the greatest—you're the least likely person He would ever use." The accuser may have kept going, "Not only did Jesus hear what you said, but all the disciples heard it too.

Now they all think that you are a coward and a failure. Remember all the grandiose thoughts and visions you had of ruling with Jesus and being the highest ruler in the kingdom of God next to Jesus. You've lost Jesus your leader. Even if Jesus gets out of this situation with the Jewish leaders, He will never want to use you. He'll probably tell you to leave the group." Luke records that Peter wept bitterly. It must have seemed to him like all the dreams and expectations that had been building up over the last three years were completely shattered.

As he was going through all these emotions, Peter learned that Jesus was sentenced to death by crucifixion and that charges were made up against Him and He was accused unjustly. Peter couldn't even stand with Him. This added to his misery. For three days after the crucifixion, Peter went through waves of emotions and despair.

On the day of the resurrection, Mary Magdalene went to the tomb and found it empty. She ran and told the disciples, and Peter and John raced to the tomb. John ran ahead, got to the tomb, and stopped, but Peter ran right into the tomb and looked. Some of the disciples were starting to believe that Jesus had risen from the dead. Peter, being emotionally drained from the previous three days, was probably in shock and must have thought, "Even if Jesus did do what He said He was going to do and rose from the dead, I denied Him. Will He still want me around?" Peter joined the rest of the disciples as they all departed, leaving behind Mary, who stayed at the tomb weeping. Then Jesus appeared to her, and she ran to tell all the disciples.

The gospel of John records Jesus appearing to the disciples twice after the resurrection and talking to them. Nothing is mentioned directly to Peter that is recorded in Scripture. I can imagine Peter thinking, "Wow! Jesus rose from the dead! He said He would do it, and He did it! Is He going to fulfill His other promises about the kingdom? Am I still a part of the promises? He still hasn't talked to me about me denying Him three times. He hasn't brought it up, so I'm not going to bring it up either!" In Peter's mind, his denial was still the elephant in the room.

## PRINCIPLE 8: HUMILITY, PART 1

Maybe Peter started to put two and two together, remembering that Jesus said that the devil was going to try to sift him like wheat, and that when he returned, he would need to strengthen his brethren. But most likely these thoughts were swirling around with all the other negative thoughts from the last few days.

Peter's head was still all over the place, so he told a few of the other disciples, "I am going fishing; time to go back to what we know." Although Jesus had been talking to them and hope was starting to come back into their hearts, there were still a lot of hazy thoughts, guilt, and shame for denying the Lord lingering over Peter like a black cloud.

They fished all night and caught nothing. Then Jesus showed up on the beach and told them to cast their nets on the right side of the boat. They did, and boom—the nets were suddenly full of fish! Looking at what happened, John realized that it was something that only Jesus could do and said, "It is the Lord!" Rather than waiting to come to shore, Peter jumped into the water and swam ashore, while the others (I'm sure) were struggling to get the overloaded nets on board. This was the third time Jesus manifested himself to the disciples since His resurrection.

They ate breakfast together and then came the moment of truth. Jesus was going to address Peter directly. I am going to paraphrase and amplify the points of the discussion. Jesus started with, "Peter, do you unconditionally love Me more than all the other disciples?" Wow! What a pointed question! Peter boasted that even if everyone else denied Jesus, he would not. He said that he was more committed to Jesus than anyone. Peter, being taken back and humbled by the situation, said, "Lord, you know I have strong affections for You." Peter admitted that he did not love Him more than the others. He was confronted with his own weakness and human frailty and admitted the truth to the Lord. The word Peter used to describe his affection for Jesus was not as strong as the word Jesus used. Jesus then stunned Peter with His response, "Then go feed My sheep." Peter must have been thinking, "Wait a minute, Jesus, You still have a place of leadership for me in the kingdom? I haven't disqualified myself?" Jesus went through this scenario with

Peter a total of three times. Just as Peter denied Jesus three times, Jesus restored him three times. Peter learned that Jesus' commitment to him was greater than his commitment to Jesus. Peter was ready to take a position in the kingdom.

# HUMILITY, PART 2—PETER'S PATH TO LEADERSHIP

During those three days after Jesus' crucifixion while He was in the grave, the brokenness and despair Peter must have been in had to be unbearable. Peter was so broken and disappointed that he was in a place where the Lord could purge him from selfish ambition, pride, and boasting. It was just the place he needed to be for the motives of his heart to be revealed and to allow God to deal with them. This is a process that we will all go through if we want to love God, walk with Him, and serve His purposes. This is a process that does not happen once, but will be continually worked in and through us by the Holy Spirit.

Jesus said in the Beatitudes, "Blessed are those who are poor in spirit, for theirs is the kingdom of heaven." The question is, "What does it mean to be poor in spirit?" The word *poor* means "to be reduced to poverty and a state of being a beggar; powerless to enrich oneself." Let's give this a complete dissection, as it relates to spirituality and the kingdom of God. It is the process of being reduced in your own estimation of yourself, your self-importance, and trusting in your abilities. It is a place where selfish desires are emptied out of you and replaced with God's desires. In Psalm 37:4 the psalmist says to "delight yourself in the Lord and He will give you the desires of your heart." I find that the more we delight in Him, the more He transforms our desires into His desires. We get reduced to a place of humility—a place of entire submission to God—where our desires become His desires.

This is the process Peter went through during those three days. He was reduced in his own estimation of himself because he was confronted with his weakness and failure. He was transferred to a place of poverty of spirit. He saw his own weakness, fragility, and faults. The world system sees this as a place not to be desired, but like so many things in the kingdom, kingdom principles work so differently! Jesus said, "Blessed are those who are poor in spirit for theirs is the kingdom," meaning that kingdom authority and principles work in and through those who are poor in spirit. When we are poor in spirit, or in a place of poverty in spirit, it means that kingdom dominion and authority is living and working in and through us.

Now Peter, the one who ran for fear of the Jewish leaders and denied Jesus, stood up in the temple for all to see. He proclaimed the lordship of Jesus on the day of Pentecost with power and authority. This same Peter was the one who spoke words of life to the beggar at the "Gate Beautiful" and he was healed. He was the one who spoke boldly to the religious leaders, so powerfully that they knew he had been with Jesus. He was the one whose shadow passed over the sick and they were healed. This man learned some truths about how to use those keys of the kingdom—and he changed the world!

There is a process that happens in all of us as we walk with God. Many would call it our sanctification process. This happens as we learn to walk in His presence and commune with Him. I have spent a lot of time mediating on Hebrews 4:12-16. Many of us have heard people preach and teach on this. We have learned the power of the spoken word, how we should speak the word of God because it is sharper than any two-edged sword and has a powerful effect.

One day I read that scripture in context and I realized that it had a much broader application. Let's review it.

> For the one who has entered His rest has himself also rested from his works, as God did from His. Therefore let us be diligent to enter that rest, so that no one will fall,

through following the same example of disobedience. For the word of God is living and active and sharper than any two-edged sword, and piercing as far as the division of soul and spirit, of both joints and marrow, and able to judge the thoughts and intentions of the heart. And there is no creature hidden from its sight, but all things are open and laid bare to the eyes of Him with whom we have to do. Therefore, since we have a great high priest who has passed through the heavens, Jesus the Son of God, let us hold fast our confession. For we do not have a high priest who cannot sympathize with our weaknesses, but One who has been tempted in all things as we are, yet without sin. Therefore let us draw near with confidence to the throne of grace, so that we may receive mercy and find grace to help in time of need (Hebrews 4:10-16).

As we read through Hebrews chapters 3 and 4, we realize that the writer is exhorting his readers not to fall short into the same unbelief as the Israelites did in the wilderness. The Israelites heard the word of God spoken and did not accept it. This started at Mount Sinai when God gave them an invitation to be a holy people, a royal priesthood, and a holy nation unto Himself. That was God's invitation for engagement! He invited them to be His bride as the prophet Jeremiah recalled (Jeremiah 2:2), and they accepted it at that time. God told them to prepare themselves because He was going to come down and visit them in three days. After three days, God came. Moses recorded that when God came, the mountain burned with fire to the heart of heaven. God is so full of love, that He can appear as fire, or one can say that the fuel that creates the image of fire is love. He was coming down to interact with His bride. The people were scared by the appearance of His presence as He talking to them. They ran back to their tents, and told Moses, "You talk to God and then tell us what He said, and we will do it." They were afraid that if they would hear the words of God themselves, they would die. When they ran back to their tents, Moses exhorted them not to, saying that the Lord was testing and trying them, that if they could come into His presence and hear His voice, they would learn to fear His name. Moses later recalled in Deuteronomy 5:28-29 (NLT) Oh, that they would always have hearts like this, that they might fear me and obey all my commands! If they did, they and their descendants would prosper forever.

As a note to the reader, I would recommend that you read Exodus chapters 19-22, and then read Deuteronomy chapters 4-6, where Moses is recalling what happened in Exodus, forty years later in his life, right before his death. In Deuteronomy, Moses was writing with forty years of experience with God to ponder what happened. I will say this: where Exodus is the letter of the Law, in Deuteronomy, Moses wants to give us the spirit of the law, and you will notice numerous mentions in Deuteronomy about loving and serving God with all your heart (passions).

From that point onward, the Israelites had trouble obeying what God said, so they never entered the rest God wanted for them. The entire generation died in the wilderness, except Joshua and Caleb. They both made what should have been a few-day's trip into a forty-year journey. So we see here that the writer of Hebrews was not just talking about us speaking the Word, he was talking about us hearing the Word spoken to us, and allowing the Word to dissect and change us. The Israelites were afraid and thought that they would die when they heard the Word, because the Word would dissect the true motives of their hearts, and once that happened, they thought that this holy God would reject them.

Their unbelief was primarily caused by their lack of understanding the love and passion God had for them. If they did not run away, God would have made a way for them, even in their weaknesses and frailties.

Let's describe how it is when the Word comes forth to us. It is like a two-edged sword that dissects. It divides the soul and spirit and exposes the thoughts and intents of the heart. The soul is your mind, intellect, and emotions. Your spirit is the real you; it's what was born again and what God breathed of Himself into you to make a living soul. God is light, and His Word brings light, so the light of His Word will allow us to see what the motives of our heart are. The heart connects the spirit to the soul. It is the source of all passion, which drives out emotions, and it is the womb of the spirit.

Let's relate this back to Peter's experience. Through his experience at the time of Jesus' crucifixion, Peter realized the true motives of his heart. He realized his weakness, frailties, and faults—and it hurt! God will always find a way to expose those things in our life, not to hurt us or embarrass us, but to perfect and mature us. All things are plain and open before God; He is just trying to get us to see it. Once we are exposed, we have a choice: run away and hide, or run to God and Jesus, the High Priest who sympathizes and empathizes with the weakness of our flesh.

Peter was at a raw place. His failures were continually before him and before all others who saw and knew what had just happened. When Jesus rose from the dead and started to appear to the disciples, Peter was still unsure of his place before Jesus and where he fit in. Should he just go back to the family fishing business or should he hang around and see if Jesus still wanted him? He was deciding whether to flee or stay.

So Jesus took Peter to a spiritual place where he could receive the mercy of God. God's mercy keeps us from what we rightfully deserve. Peter deserved to be rejected and not have any part in the kingdom; after all, he rejected Jesus. But Jesus gave Peter mercy that led him into the throne of grace. How did Jesus do this? By turning around Peter's former assertion about loving Jesus more than everyone else (thinking he deserved a position and calling in the kingdom) and asking him, "Do you unconditionally love Me, and by that, I mean, are you more committed to Me than all the others?" I can imagine Peter taking a big gulp and thinking, "How I should answer that?" Peter replied, "I have strong affections for You." Peter did something very important—he admitted the truth. He did have strong affections for Jesus, but not more love and commitment to Him than to the others.

The door to the grace of God started opening to Peter. Grace is God's willingness to use His ability and power on our behalf to bring on us what we cannot bring on ourselves, even though we don't deserve it. Peter showed humility by admitting the truth. Humility happens when we see and admit the truth about ourselves and God. God gives grace to the humble; He brings us right into His presence and to His throne where we can receive from Him. Although we can receive mercy any time, we need to find grace. Grace is only found by humility, which we demonstrate not by running *from* God, but rather running *to* Him, admitting the truth, and seeking Him for grace to be transformed and changed.

Peter and Jesus went through this three times, which parallels Peter's three denials of Jesus. At the end of each of these, Jesus tells Peter, "Go feed My sheep." Peter learned that his position in the kingdom was not based on his works or commitment to God, but rather based on grace and his response to that grace. Jesus did not say, "Go rule My kingdom." He said, "Feed My sheep."

I can see the grace of God flooding Peter's soul and transforming him. He understood the corruption of his own soul as well as the grace of God that changed him, bringing him to a place where he could be an effective vessel in His kingdom.

It was during the latter end of Peter's life and ministry when he wrote 2 Peter. He was exhorting the other pastors, elders, and leaders to feed the Word to God's flock. Not just the written Word of God, but the words of God that brings life; words that are a daily revelation; words that are breathed by the spirit of truth. Not leading them by force to do what we want or leading them for the financial benefits we can get by being a leader. When we do this as leaders, it is called building our own kingdom rather than building God's kingdom.

Peter writes that we cannot operate like the worldly leaders. Doesn't this sound like what Jesus told them: that leadership in the kingdom is not like how earthly leaders do things? (Matthew 20:25-28; Luke 22:25-

## HUMILITY, PART 2—PETER'S PATH TO LEADERSHIP

27) Peter writes that we need to be an example, a pattern. Paul said the same thing, "Be followers of me as I am of Christ." True godliness and Christlikeness will attract those who want and are interested in God.

Then Peter exhorted the people to be in subjection to the leaders and the leaders to be in subjection to them, meaning we are all accountable to one another. The term *subjection* has both a military and non-military meaning. From a military point of view, it means to arrange military troops under the full control of a leader. Like the Centurion who explained to Jesus that when he would tell his men to go, they would go, and to come and they would come. In a non-military fashion, subjection meant an attitude of voluntary giving and submission to one another cooperating with one another, each caring and assuming the responsibility and burden of each other. In this context of the scripture, we read that leaders are not supposed to lord it over people in a way that forces them to do what they want. So the only logical meaning for *subjection* here is in the non-military fashion.

If we think about Peter's progression and spiritual growth, he went from selfish ambition, to vying for the highest position in Jesus' kingdom, to boasting that he would never deny Jesus, to fulfilling Jesus' prophecy about denying Him, to despair and hopelessness. Jesus returns and lets Peter know that there is still a place for him in His kingdom. From there Peter goes on to preaching the first sermon after the day of Pentecost and leading many to the Lord and having a fruitful life and ministry. It was humility that worked in him and transformed him through the grace of God. He came around as the Holy Spirit revealed to him how the kingdom works, how the kingdom gets advanced. The things he saw Jesus do and the words He said came alive in Peter. Then as we read through the book of Acts we see how the influence of the kingdom worked through Peter and changed things in the world around him.

Let's move forward to the day of Pentecost in Acts 2, Peter preaching after the outpouring of the Holy Spirit when three-thousand souls were added to the kingdom. Acts records that there was a scene of awe among the people, and many signs and wonders were done by the hands of the apostles. In Acts 3 we read about the lame beggar at the Gate Beautiful being healed when Peter gazed on him and said to him, "Silver and gold I have none, but such as I have I give unto you, rise and walk," and immediately the beggar stood up and walked. All the people saw this and praised God. Then Peter preached his second sermon and five-thousand people met Jesus that day. We probably don't need to go on from here, but in the book of Acts we can see the authority of the Lion working in the meekness of the Lamb, affecting the world around Peter for the kingdom of God. We see this in both Peter's works and in his writing. If you read the book of Acts and the two epistles he wrote, you will see glimpses of revelations from the teachings he heard from Jesus about becoming living epistles.

# HUMILITY, PART 3— DWELLING WITH GOD

One Sunday evening before preaching in a worship service, I was sitting next to a young man. He leaned over to me and said, "God wants me to go higher." He was obviously sincere, and I could see that God was moving in him. He asked me what that meant. I answered him, but didn't feel that the answer I gave him was complete. A few days later I was thinking about that situation, and the Lord asked me, "Do you know what it means to go higher?" I realized what the Lord was saying, when He said, "I want you to go higher in me, it meant that I needed to go lower." It is such a recurring theme throughout the Word of God. Jesus said that he who exalts himself shall be humbled, and he who humbles himself shall be exalted. It sounds nice and good when we all say that we want to go higher in God, but the reality of it costs you something. It is the death of you, death of self-dependence, and a reduction to a place of complete dependence on God. Jesus said it another way: He who loses his life shall really gain life.

I started to recall scriptures throughout the Bible that talked about humility and going lower. One that stood out was Isaiah 57:15 (NLT), which says:

> The high and lofty one who lives in eternity, the Holy One, says this: "I live in the high and holy place with those whose spirits are contrite and humble. I restore the

crushed spirit of the humble and revive the courage of those with repentant hearts.

He is the highest God, the highest of the high—meaning there is no one higher or holier than him. God transcends all measurement of everything; there is no one higher than him in knowledge, wisdom, love, kindness, goodness, mercy, truth, perfect judgment, or anything else we would want to measure. That is why He is holy. God is so holy that the living creatures that sit around His throne and behold Him are covered with eyes all around and within. These are not natural eyes but spiritual eyes.

The question begs to be asked, "Why do they have all these eyes?" They have these eyes to comprehend His holiness. They are constantly crying "holy" because continually, throughout all eternity, they see and understand something new about the characteristics of His holiness. They don't cry "holy" because God makes them cry "holy," they cry "holy" because they cannot help themselves. Every moment they see a new transcendent holy characteristic that is a part of who God is. In a moment, they see something new about His love that they have never seen before, so they cry "holy." In another moment, they see new mercy that they never saw before, so they cry "holy." This goes on and on.

We read in Isaiah 6 that when Isaiah saw the Lord, he saw angels who were crying "holy" and saying that all the earth was filled with His glory. Their voices were so powerful and passionate that it shook the doorposts of the temple they were in. Isaiah was completely in awe. He was completely undone and exposed in the presence of God, and he could not hide. In a moment of time, all the inner most thoughts and desires of his heart were exposed before God. He knew that God saw his inmost weakness, frailties, and sins. He cried out and said that he was undone and exposed. Then God sent a coal from the altar to cleanse him, which we see now represents the cleansing and transforming power of the cross.

God inhabits eternity; that is the place where eternal life is. It is both a quality and quantity of life. It's a place where sin does not exist, a place

## HUMILITY, PART 3—DWELLING WITH GOD

where there is no destruction; it is where God dwells. In John 17:3, Jesus said that eternal life is to know the only true God and Jesus the Christ who God sent. Eternal life is experienced with a personal revelation and understanding of the Father and the Son, which is revealed in the person of the Holy Spirit.

God says that He dwells, or lives, with the contrite and the humble, and that He will revive their spirit and hearts. To revive means to make alive and live prosperously. When God's life comes into us, we start to live the life that was meant to be.

There is something regarding the humble and contrite in heart that puts us in a place of fellowship and interaction with God. It is a place where you understand that the plans of man, the ways of man, and the strength of man at his best does not result in the outcome of what God wants us to do. There are many well-meaning men and woman of God who have gotten a revelation of God's purposes for their life and have seen God's call on their life and understood that God's kingdom needs to be established on the earth.

These people may have set out in a well-meaning effort to do so. You can know in general the plans and purposes of God, but very easily allow worldly methods, or as Paul says, carnal methods, of accomplishing those things to enter in and direct us. We think we are doing God's work, but the methods of accomplishing those things are worldly and fleshy—and the result is the destruction of the spiritual lives of the very people we are trying to help.

Let me give you a few examples from the Bible. Let's start with Moses. At forty years old, Moses knew that there was a calling on his life to deliver his brethren. He probably felt this burden and passion and wanted to do something. So he went to visit them. He found an Egyptian soldier mistreating one of his brethren, so he stepped in and killed the Egyptian soldier. Shortly thereafter, he realized that that was not the path God had chosen, and he had to flee. He ended up on the other side of the desert for forty years. He went from the highest place in worldly honor to tending sheep as a shepherd. According to Stephen's account of Moses in his defense before he was stoned, he said that Moses was an eloquent man, mighty in word and deed (Acts 7:22). When Moses met God at the burning bush on Mt. Sinai, God told him to go and talk to Pharaoh and tell him to let His people go. Moses said that he could not do it. He was slow of tongue; he was a stutterer. Moses went through a place of brokenness, where hopelessness probably set in and left him wondering how God could use him. The reality is that we need to get to a place of understanding how to walk and dwell with God. God took Moses and revived his heart and spirit, then sent him to the work that he was called to do.

What about Abraham? God promised him a son who would be his heir; the chosen child. He said this son would start the seed of his lineage and that there would be more of them than the sands of the sea. God gave Abraham this promise when he was seventy-five years old. So it is easy to believe for an older man to have a child, but for an older woman to have a child would have to be a miracle. The years went by and nothing happened. Then one day Abram's wife, Sarai, had an idea. If God was not able to do this, He needed help. Abram listened to her and took her servant Hagar and they had a son, Ishmael. But a few years later God moved supernaturally and Grandma Sarai, whose name is now a covenant name of Sarah, conceived and brought forth Isaac. Throughout all history, and even today there has been strife between the seed of Ishmael and the seed of Isaac. Almost all the countries in the Middle East grew out of the seed of Isaac or the seed of Ishmael. They are still fighting today, even though they are brothers and born from the same lineage. Paul writes about this in Galatians 4:

> For it is written that Abraham had two sons, one by the bondwoman and one by the free woman. But the son by the bondwoman was born according to the flesh and the son by the free woman through the promise (Galatians 4:22-23).

## HUMILITY, PART 3—DWELLING WITH GOD

It does not mean that God loves the Arab nations any less, but the works of the flesh produce flesh. Spiritual death cannot produce spiritual life. We cannot perform the will of God based on the wisdom of man.

After learning these lessons Abram, now called Abraham, followed God's direction when he was told to sacrifice the promised child, Isaac, and did it exactly as God said. As a result of this act of faith, God provided His own sacrifice that day instead of Isaac. Later, Jesus was sent to be the real sacrifice for our sins. Abraham was then called the father of faith, and his acts were used as an example of death for all of history. Even though Abraham was the "father of faith" according to Romans chapter 4, he still made mistakes. But in spite of his mistakes, God saw that Abraham came to a place of complete submission and He breathed life into him, causing the plans of God to be fulfilled in the earth.

The accounts of Peter and the other eleven apostles, as discussed earlier in the book, are just other examples of learning how to understand and walk in the plans of God. After Peter went through his time of great trial and despair after denying the Lord, God sent a great outpouring of the Holy Spirit upon mankind through Peter. We see in Acts 2 that Peter stood up with boldness and preached Christ. In Acts 3, we see that the man at Gate Beautiful was healed, again there was another outpouring of God's Spirit upon the people, with Peter as the primary vessel. In Acts 5, we see the signs and wonders that were performed through Peter even as his shadow passed over the sick. God revived the spirit of people. He revived the hearts of the broken. Peter learned something about humility, meekness, brokenness, and dwelling in the presence of God.

Revelation chapter 3 reveals this concept. When Jesus is talking to John about the seven churches, Laodicea, the last church, was the only church that did not receive a commendation from Jesus. It was this church that Jesus addressed as lukewarm. But the question is, why did Jesus call them lukewarm? Let's see what Jesus said:

> I know all the things you do, that you are neither hot nor cold. I wish that you were one or the other! But since you are like lukewarm water, neither hot nor cold, I will spit you out of my mouth! You say, "I am rich. I have everything I want. I don't need a thing!" And you don't realize that you are wretched and miserable and poor and blind and naked. So I advise you to buy gold from me—gold that has been purified by fire. Then you will be rich. Also buy white garments from me so you will not be shamed by your nakedness and ointment for your eyes so you will be able to see. I correct and discipline everyone I love. So be diligent and turn from your indifference.
>
> Look! I stand at the door and knock. If you hear my voice and open the door, I will come in, and we will share a meal together as friends. Those who are victorious will sit with me on my throne, just as I was victorious and sat with my Father on his throne.
>
> Anyone with ears to hear must listen to the Spirit and understand what he is saying to the churches (Revelation 3:15-22 NLT).

Jesus told the church that they were lukewarm. We know that lukewarm water is so distasteful that we tend to spit it out. Too often, we assume that the term *lukewarm* is only centered around the works and commitment that we have toward the works of God. We don't pray enough. We don't study the Word enough. We don't witness enough. It is the path of not doing enough. I don't want to belittle that there are things we should do based on the inspiration of the Holy Spirit and the Word of God, but that is not the reason Jesus said the Laodiceans were lukewarm. He said that they were lukewarm because the people of Laodicea said that they have no need for Jesus, meaning that they were self-dependent and they had everything they needed. We can think our works are enough, but if our works are not born out of communion, dependence, and inspiration of God, they are only works. Human compassion and works are sometimes

## HUMILITY, PART 3—DWELLING WITH GOD

just a substitution for living a life in submission to God and the power of the cross.

The Laodiceans trusted in their riches. Their riches brought self-confidence and dependence on themselves rather than on God. There is so much in the Word of God that talks about not trusting in riches. In the book of Deuteronomy (8:12-18), Moses warns the children of Israel that when they have built homes and have had many flocks and their gold and silver is multiplied, they are not to become proud. They were not to think that it was their own power or strength that brought them their wealth and success, but they needed to remember that it was from God:

> But you shall remember the LORD your God, for it is He who is giving you power to make wealth, that He may confirm His covenant which He swore to your fathers, as it is this day (Deuteronomy 8:18).

Paul tells Timothy in 2 Timothy 6 to not trust in the uncertainty of riches, but in the living God who gives us richly all things to enjoy.

Laodicea was known for its wealth and commerce. It was a very well-off city. There was a large manufacturing industry for woolen carpets and cloth. They also had a very wealthy banking system and medical school known for ointments that could be applied on the eyes and ears. Jesus said that He knew their works, so on the surface they may have been doing many works that could be perceived as things they should do because of their faith in Christ. But as I have come to know God, I have learned that He is not concerned with how we look and how we are perceived outwardly. Rather, He looks at the motivation of the heart and why we are doing what we are doing. Do we do it to look good, or do we do it because we love God and love the people of God? Paul writes that we are all going to be judged for the things done in the body, whether good or evil. As I have meditated on that, I have come to realize that the core motivation behind our works should be to love God and love His people.

When I think of Jesus wanting to spit the Laodiceans out of His mouth, I have thoughts of the description earlier in the book of Revelation that says that there was fire in His eyes and a sword in His mouth. I picture Jesus trying to commune and fellowship with His people, wanting to dwell in them, guide them, and communicate with them, but them not resisting communing with Him and listening to His voice. In response, Jesus just backs off and allows them to do what they think is right in their own eyes.

One day while I was worshipping in church, the Lord drew my attention to this scripture. He gave me a picture of what Jesus was saying about spitting the lukewarm out of His mouth. He gave me a picture of two lovers embracing and kissing. One of the lovers realized that the other had no passion in their affection and embrace for them. That lover was hurt because the other lover did not respond to the embrace and love that was being passionately given out. The other lover was just going through the motions. The lover who was passionately showing affection later felt like spitting because the experience was so distasteful.

One of the most treacherous places in our lives is when things are going well in most areas, or if you have just had a great victory or accomplishment. It can be easy to lose sight of dependence on the living God and the communion and fellowship we have with Him that we desperately need. We think that because everything is going well, we must be in the will of God and God's blessings are on our life. But we never really know that until we have intimate fellowship and communion with Him.

Sometimes this deception happens because we judge our spirituality by the works we perform: the attendance we have at our assembly, the doctrines we know, the things we say, and the way we act outwardly. Jesus gave a solution for this in Revelation 3. He told them to buy gold that is refined in the fire. Gold represents the purity of the divine nature. Fire is a description of the living God. God is described as a consuming fire in Exodus, and that fact is reiterated in the book of Hebrews. That fire purifies us and purifies all that separates us from God. It exposes the true thoughts and intents of our hearts and leads us into a place of union and agreement with God. The fuel to God's fire is His love, it purifies us. In the book of Revelation, Jesus is described with fire proceeding from His eyes.

We cannot see the fire from His eyes unless we come into His presence and seek His face. Once we seek His face, it does something to us. It allows us to see things the way He does. It discerns the true thoughts and intents of the heart and exposes all the impurities of the flesh.

The writer of Hebrews talks about this in chapter 4. He says that the word of God is living and active and sharper than any two-edged sword, dividing the soul and spirit and able to judge the thoughts and intents of the heart. The truth behind this scripture is not just speaking the word of God, but us hearing the word of God, and allowing the word to access our hearts.

When this happens, all things are exposed for what they are. The writer of Hebrews says that all things are naked and open. This means that we are coming to God naked and open, not hiding anything from Him; we are completely exposed. When we are completely exposed before God, He clothes us with His glory. We can choose to have God clothe us, or we can choose to clothe ourselves. We can hide from God as Adam and Eve did, trying to clothe their nakedness, or come to God and allow Him to transform and clothe us with His clothing.

Jesus said to the church, "I stand at the door and knock." We normally use this text for calling people to Christ in order to receive salvation. However, here Jesus is talking to believers in the church and asking the church to let Him in. Jesus stands at the door of their hearts and knocks; He is always knocking and trying to have communion and interaction with the heart of man. The (spiritual) heart of man is the womb of the spirit. It is where the word is sown (according to the parable of the sower in Matthew 13:19), it is the source of all passions and emotions (Proverbs 4:23), and it is the joining place of the spirit to the soul (Hebrews 4:12). As He continually has access to our heart, He transforms us and we come into union with Him and understand His ways and thoughts. We realize that all human strength and wisdom will never produce the works of God. I think Paul referred to all human works and accomplishments as dung in his letter to the Philippian church (Philippians 3). The result of this process is that it allows us to sit with Jesus on His throne in heaven, as He sits on the throne of our hearts.

Thrones represent authority and power. Can you see the picture here? We humble ourselves before God and come to the throne of grace as we fellowship and interact with Him. Here we receive mercy, which keeps us from what we rightfully deserve, and then we find grace to give us what we don't deserve. We can receive the authority of the Lion and we have union and communion with the Lamb.

This is the process Peter went through during his time of sifting when he denied the Lord and when the Lord came back and restored him. He was restored to his position and calling and walked in fellowship with the Lord. Then he lived in the authority of the kingdom—all of which was demonstrated in the books of Acts. As a note here, this process is not a one-time transformation. It is a lifelong process of continually being transformed by going lower in yourself and then going higher in the kingdom.

# PRINCIPLE 9: THE CROSS— THE GREATEST MYSTERY OF THE KINGDOM

When Jesus was teaching His disciples, He taught them in parables, and the greatest of the parables was the parable of the sower. Jesus said that if you cannot understand this parable, you cannot understand any of the parables, meaning that the spiritual truths communicated in the parable of the sower was essential for understanding all other parables.

> And He said to them, "Do you not understand this parable? How will you understand all the parables? (Mark 4:13).

As He spoke to them about the parable of the sower, He said, "Also to you has been granted to know the mysteries of the kingdom." A mystery is a secret spiritual truth, not obvious to worldly understanding. The greatest of these mysteries that God the Father planned with the agreement of God the Son, was the work of the cross that brought redemption to man. The cross was the attack weapon of the kingdom. We may not think of the cross as an attack weapon. This was the channel through which God was able to gain access to the keys of hell, death, and the grave, ultimately providing the keys of the kingdom.

I want to make a note here which I will explain later. There are two sets of keys that Jesus mentioned: one in Matthew 16 and the other in Revelation 2. They are different sets of keys for different purposes. But the design plan of the cross was the medium through which both were obtained. Jesus took the keys of death, hell, and grave, and they can never be taken away from Him. This brought back the eternal redemption of man. Once man was eternally redeemed, God could provide him the keys of His kingdom.

The first thing the cross did was release mankind from the bondages of sin that lead to spiritual death. This spiritual death led man to a place where he could be dominated and influenced by the evil one, with very little ability to overcome him.

Jesus was in His earthly ministry for three years, and during that time, the evil one and the evil forces released by the rulers of this world could not stop or hinder him. Their twisting of Old Testament scriptures with the help of the Pharisees in order to trick Him was fruitless. Hence, they stopped trying because their motives and intents where completely exposed by Jesus. When they would try to seize Jesus, either He would walk right through them or they would be so taken by His words. It seemed that the more they tried to entrap Him, the more popular Jesus became, and the more miracles He did, and the more influence He had on people.

From Adam to the time of Jesus' death, the evil one had the power of death and the grave. Every person who died during that period went to the lower parts of the earth or hell. At this time, there were two places. One was for the righteous who had righteousness imparted unto them and were waiting to be released. The others, however, went to the place where there was great suffering and pain.

A plan was devised to kill Jesus. By killing Him, His natural life would leave and He would no longer have any influence on the earth and in the hearts of men. Not knowing that this was the plan of God, they crucified Jesus. Just think about how the plan of God worked. In the worldly

## PRINCIPLE 9: THE CROSS—THE GREATEST MYSTERY OF THE KINGDOM

sense, shedding of blood would release the life that was in the body and incur death. Then the spirit would be ushered to the lower parts of the earth or hell (hades), where there were two compartments according to the story Jesus told in Luke 16:20-25. But the cross was the place where Jesus shed His blood and His natural body died. He was then ushered into the lower parts of the earth. In Ephesians 4:9, Paul says that Jesus descended to the lower parts. This act was the greatest "Trojan Horse" in all of history—the Son of God was down in the lower parts of hades in the presence of the evil one and all his minions. For three days the mighty Son of God who thwarted every work of hell on earth was in the midst of His enemy, being taunted and scorned. He was acting as the scapegoat, which was the second animal offered on the Day of Atonement (see Leviticus 16:10). But suddenly, while the workers of hell were rejoicing and torturing the Son of God, the Father said, "That is enough." Because Jesus never sinned, but offered Himself willingly as a sacrifice for sin, when the Father spoke, it released the Holy Spirit and the glory of the Father entered into the gates of hell (Romans 6:4). Then God breathed life back into Jesus and raised Him up again amid all the forces of hell. By shedding His life, He regained our life. His was the sacrifice that paid the penalty of sin and became sin itself. He was our substitute.

Paul writes about this in 1 Corinthians 2:6-8:

> Yet we do speak wisdom among those who are mature; a wisdom, however, not of this age nor of the rulers of this age, who are passing away; but we speak God's wisdom in a **mystery, the hidden wisdom which God predestined before the ages to our glory; the wisdom which none of the rulers of this age has understood; for if they had understood it they would not have crucified the Lord of glory.**

Just think of the day of Pentecost on earth when the Holy Spirit came in like a rushing mighty wind and created a great disruption on earth. I picture Jesus being in the lower parts of earth, bearing the penalty of sin—not just as the sacrificial lamb, but as the scapegoat who was sent into the wilderness to take away man's sins and be devoured by the predators of the land. The Holy Spirit came there. I picture the Holy Spirit approaching hell and every foundation and every being in hell wondering what was going on. Never before had they seen this in hell! The pillar of fire appears. The rushing mighty wind blasts its way in, resting upon Jesus, and the Father says, "Let there be light." The power of the living God raises Jesus from the dead. Jesus walks over to the devil and takes back the keys of death and the grave, never to be taken again.

This day had to be one of the devil's worst nightmares. He thought he had defeated the Son of God. With Him captive, he thought he still had authority on earth, death, hell, and the grave. The Father made Jesus, the righteous Son of God, to be sin—He who knew no sin, in order that we might become righteous. He exchanged His righteousness for our sin. We became righteous, and He became sin. This is why Jesus said, "My God, My God, why have you forsaken me?" Because Jesus never willingly sinned and in humility and meekness submitted to the will of the Father, God the Father breathed life back into Jesus through the Holy Spirit. Jesus submitted Himself in humble obedience to the Father as a sacrifice for sin, paid the penalty of sin, and suffered for our sin.

Through death and the shedding of His life and his blood, He reclaimed the power over death and destroyed the devil who had authority over death. Think of this: it was the exact opposite way anyone (except for God) could have conceived it. The rulers of the world, both spiritual and natural, had no comprehension of the awesome work or process.

We read below in Revelation 1:17-18 how Jesus, through His death and then victory, was able to take the keys of death and Hades.

> When I saw Him, I fell at His feet like a dead man. And He placed His right hand on me, saying, "Do not be afraid; I am the first and the last, and the living One; **and I was dead, and behold, I am alive forevermore, and I have the keys of death and of Hades**.

## PRINCIPLE 9: THE CROSS—THE GREATEST MYSTERY OF THE KINGDOM

Jesus took the keys of death and hades back so He could lead all the righteous who were in Abraham bosom, according to Matthew 27:51-51. When Jesus was raised from the dead, the righteous saints of old were seen in the streets and they entered into the Holy City and appeared to many people.

Jesus the Christ delivered us from the power of death. Paul so thoroughly tells us in the book of Romans (chapters 1-8), how sin reigned from Adam to Moses, even in those who did not sin in the likeness of the offense of Adam. In Genesis, Adam and Eve were told that if they were to eat of the Tree of the Knowledge of Good and Evil, they would die, or literally it says, "in dying they will die." They separated themselves from life, communion, and fellowship with God. They received the knowledge of evil. With this knowledge, the evil one could influence them toward evil, especially without the life of God leading them toward good.

Moses instituted the Law, which provided a covering for their sins. It was weak because it was just an outer expression of the flesh and man's inner being could not be changed. Paul tells us that through the gift of righteousness and the abundance of grace, we will reign in authority of Christ. The work of the spirit of life in Christ has set us free from the law of sin and death. So a wonderful work happened at the cross! The God of heaven provided the power to redeem and transform man. The moment we say yes to Jesus and His works, God says in our innermost being, "light be." The old dead man is put to death; the new man is created by the life of God. We become united with Jesus in His work, His crucifixion, His death, His burial, His quickening (being made alive again), His resurrection, and His exaltation. Paul says that we were united in His death and we shall also be united in His resurrection. Once we are made clean and whole by the work of the cross, we are translated out of the kingdom of darkness and transferred into the kingdom of His beloved Son.

Jesus's work on the cross is the holiest and most powerful act of all human history. In all of heaven and earth, history is centered around the cross. There was enough power in the cross to redeem all of mankind for all eternity. Now the question is, how does such great power get released? It was released in humble obedience of the Son because it was the will of the Father.

Think of what was written in Philippians 2:6-11 (NLT) by the Apostle Paul:

> Though he was God, he did not think of equality with God as something to cling to. Instead, he gave up his divine privileges; he took the humble position of a slave and was born as a human being. When he appeared in human form, he humbled himself in obedience to God and died a criminal's death on a cross. Therefore, God elevated Him to the place of highest honor and gave Him the name above all other names, that at the name of Jesus every knee should bow, in heaven and on earth and under the earth, and every tongue confess that Jesus Christ is Lord, to the glory of God the Father.

The greatest victory over evil, the greatest release of heavenly power was accomplished by the meekness and humility of Jesus the Christ. Let's look at the depth of His humility. First, Jesus was at the right hand of the Father and was an equal partner with the Father. For him to do what the Father asked, He had to not count the glory, honor, power, blessing, wisdom, and authority that He had as the ultimate prize and fulfillment of His being. So if He didn't count that the prize, then what was the prize? The prize was doing the will of the Father; and the will of the Father was redeeming fallen man. God counted mankind as the prize. I know this may be hard to comprehend, but you need to say, "God the Father and God the Son counted me as the PRIZE!"

So God himself stepped out of eternity in the form of a man. To do this He had to be born as a human and experience entrance into this world in human form. The incorruptible seed of the Father entered the womb of Mary, and she conceived the God-man. He was Jesus in His Humanity and Christ in His deity. He was born in the humblest of human places—a

## PRINCIPLE 9: THE CROSS—THE GREATEST MYSTERY OF THE KINGDOM

manger. He lived a humble obscure life in an obscure town. Then at the proper time, God sent Him forth in His ministry. He was filled with the Holy Spirit and He only did the works that He saw the Father do. In His earthy ministry, He did the greatest works a man could perform for man: Healing the sick, raising the dead, restoring sight to the blind, as well as speaking words that no man has ever spoken before.

His earthly ministry and influence were growing. Men were seeing Him as the Messiah, and people thought that this was how God the Father was going to restore the kingdom of David. When the religious leaders would try to take Him, He would walk right through them; when they tried to trap Him by twisting the law, His words were so filled with heavenly wisdom that they stopped trying to trap Him because it only made them look foolish and appear jealous of Him.

When He was at the height of His ministry and popularity He started talking about going to the cross and being mistreated, beaten, and killed by the religious leaders. Peter was so totally perplexed by these statements that He rebuked Jesus. Jesus gave Peter an uncompromising rebuke back, telling Satan to get behind Him and not to think of things that are just in his best interest.

Jesus humbled Himself as a man. Though the people wanted to make Him a king, He did not take the glory of man and what they wanted to give Him. He gave Himself up willingly to the religious leaders. He allowed the devil to inspire the people to hatred and resulted in the sentence of death on the cross.

Jesus humbled himself, shed the heavenly glory of God, and became man. Then as man, He rejected the power of the kingdom of man that man and the devil wanted to give Him. In His humility and meekness, He accepted the will of the Father, which was to go to the cross and suffer pain and shed His blood for the redemption of man. So through the internal virtues of humility and meekness demonstrated through His offering on the cross, the greatest exaltation with power was released on the earth since it's creation.

Paul said it best in Philippians 2:8-11 (NLT):

> He humbled himself in obedience to God and died a criminal's death on a cross. Therefore, God elevated him to the place of highest honor and gave him the name above all other names, that at the name of Jesus every knee should bow, in heaven and on earth and under the earth, and every tongue confess that Jesus Christ is Lord, to the glory of God the Father.

In the heavenlies, seen as recorded by John in Revelation 5:12-14 (NLT):

> "Worthy is the Lamb who was slaughtered—
> to receive power and riches
> and wisdom and strength
> and honor and glory and blessing."
> And then I heard every creature in heaven and on earth
> and under the earth and in the sea. They sang:
> "Blessing and honor and glory and power
> belong to the one sitting on the throne
> and to the Lamb forever and ever."
> And the four living beings said, "Amen!"
> And the twenty-four elders fell down and worshiped
> the Lamb.

When the work was done, this authority and power was released on earth. Since creation, such light had not been manifested on the earth. Paul says it so eloquently in his letter to the Corinthians in 2 Corinthians 4:6, the God who said "let there be light," or "light be." This is a reference to creation when the light of God's presence was released into a world that was formless and void (Genesis 1). God said, "light be" or "let there be light in the hearts of man," and the light of God's power shone in our hearts and transferred the power of the cross into the spirit of man and recreated his inner being into the image and likeness of God. No longer was our spirit dead, formless, and void, but the life of God was

## PRINCIPLE 9: THE CROSS—THE GREATEST MYSTERY OF THE KINGDOM

imparted back to us. The keys of death, hell, and the grave were taken back eternally for man, and man was given a new kingdom to live in and was provided with keys to access the authority of that kingdom.

# THE POWER OF THE CROSS—ANOTHER KEY OF THE KINGDOM

Although Jesus' work on the cross is done and we don't have to do the same work Jesus did as an offering for sin and dying on the cross, we must in similitude take up our cross in humble communion and union with Him.

This is what Jesus talked about several times in the Gospels. The most notable was in Matthew 16, where Peter received a great commendation for confessing that Jesus was the Christ. Jesus told them that they were going to get the keys of the kingdom and whatever they bound on earth shall be bound in heaven and whatever they loose on earth shall be loosed in heaven.

Jesus went on to tell them of His suffering that was going to happen at the hands of the religious leaders, that He was going to be killed and then rise from the dead. The disciples had no understanding of what Jesus was talking about. All Peter heard was that Jesus was going to die. If the King of the new kingdom died, how would they receive their position and authority? So Peter (either knowingly or unknowingly) rebuked Jesus. Well, we know how that went. Jesus turned to Peter and said, "Get behind me, Satan." Peter had to think, "Did He just call me Satan? I was trying to protect and help Him."

Peter was thinking of his own self-interests. His self-interests were in direct contrast to God's. Peter wanted the kingdom to come and wanted the will of God to be done. Just like Peter, many of us are misled by our own natural understanding of how God accomplishes His plans, so we rely on carnal understanding and methods.

Jesus told him that he must take up his cross and follow Him. Thinking about the timing of this statement, Jesus still had not gone to the cross, and they were all familiar with the Roman practice of crucifixion. So this should have created much concern in their minds. What the heck was Jesus talking about? How could they lose their life in order to find it? If you die, your life ends on earth. How do you lose your life and then find the life that God has for you?

I think that later they must have realized that to gain their leadership and authority with earthly methods, they would lose their soul. The question is: Why is it if they use worldly methods they will not succeed? Because when they do that it is diametrically opposed to the ways of God. John tells us in 1 John about what is in the world: the lust of the flesh, lust of the eyes, and the boastful pride of life—and these things will not last. These cause you to lose your soul because the guiding force of your soul is the wisdom that comes from the life of God. When selfish desires of the flesh come in, they cause us to act in ways that sacrifice everything for our best interests, causing confusion, contention, strife, jealousy, and anger. These all lead to destruction of our lives and the lives of those around us.

I can see how the disciples had no idea what Jesus was talking about. I can picture them thinking, "There He goes again, talking about things we have no clue about." But once Jesus went to the cross and was raised and they saw His willing sacrifice, they finally started to understand what He was talking about.

Then Paul came along and started describing what happened from the cross to the throne: the new birth, and the access to the life of God as a result of Christ's substitutionary work. Once we identify with it

## THE POWER OF THE CROSS—ANOTHER KEY OF THE KINGDOM

and receive it, we receive the results of it without performing the work it entails.

But our cross is to lay down our desires, ways, and ambitions to follow the desires, ways, and ambitions of God the Father in our life. That's why Jesus told us to pray for His kingdom to come on earth (in us) and that His will be done in heaven.

Paul writes in the New Testament that like Jesus was crucified, so we are crucified; as Jesus died, we died; as Jesus was buried, we are buried; as Jesus was quickened or made alive, we are quickened or made alive; as Jesus was raised from the dead, we are raised from the dead; and as Jesus is seated in heavenly places, we are seated in heavenly places. Positional in Christ, all these things have happened to us and God sees us as He sees Christ. We need to walk in humility and meekness to deny ourselves and allow the work of the cross to live in us, so in our daily experience, we can position ourselves in Christ. Paul writes that as we are crucified with Christ, the life we live in the flesh is the life of God in us (Galatians 2:20), that we walk in newness of life (Romans 6:4), and when Christ, who is our life, is revealed in us, then we are revealed in His glory (Colossians 3:4). Paul also gives insight into his spiritual life in Philippians 3 that he has not attained these things yet, but he presses on to the goal of the prize of the high (or above) calling of God in Christ Jesus. I love the way Paul puts it—he presses on that he may know Him, the power of His resurrection, and the fellowship of His sufferings, that in these things he would be conformed in His death so that he may attain the place of the resurrection of the dead. The place of the resurrection of the dead literally spells out "resurrection." This is the place where we walk in our daily experience, what we are in our position in Christ, and where we are seated in order to reign with Him in heavenly places.

Paul knew that the secret of his life and transformation was hidden in the cross. That is why when he came to the Corinthian church and when they were bickering, he said, "I determined to know nothing among you except Jesus Christ, and him crucified." His trust was in the cross and the power of God, not eloquent words, (1 Corinthians 2:1-4). Paul also said that he would glory only in the cross of the Lord Jesus Christ by which He was crucified to the world and the world to Him (Galatians 6:14).

I was meditating on these two verses one day during a very difficult time of my life. God showed me that the answer to dealing with these difficult things was hidden in the cross. I realized that the cross was like a heavenly force field that could keep us from the effects of the world. As Paul would keep his life focused on the cross, it would transform him, strengthen him, and keep him from the evil desires and passions of selfishness that try to creep in from the world.

As time went on, I started to realize the power of the cross, or the crucified life—the life that denies our selfish ambition and desires that can so easily corrupt the most spiritual people. One day while I was in worship and prayer, God gave me a revelation of the cross. I saw a very powerful lightning bolt hit a tree. We know what happens then. The tree gets obliterated, starts to burn, and gets destroyed. The tree cannot be a conductor of the power of the lightning bolt; the lightning bolt is too powerful for the tree. The Lord showed me that the tree was like a spiritually dead man; God's power and life would destroy a sinful spiritually-dead man.

Then I saw myself on a cross which was made from wood, and a similar lightning bolt hit the cross. But instead of destroying the cross and me, I absorbed the power of the lightning bolt and became a conductor of that power. So when I hide my life in the cross, the power of God will work in me and transform me to become a conductor of the life of heaven. Taking up my cross, denying myself and my selfish ambitions, and submitting to the perfect loving will of the Father allows me to live the most powerful and fulfilling life there is—a life full of His presence and glory. In His presence is fullness of joy and in His right hand are pleasures forever.

Paul was stating in Colossians chapter 3 that he had died in Christ and his life is hidden with Christ in God, and when Christ's life is revealed, we shall be revealed with Him in glory. The more we internalize and

## THE POWER OF THE CROSS—ANOTHER KEY OF THE KINGDOM

come to understand the power of the cross, the more the glory of the living God has its way in us, and the more we walk in the authority of the kingdom. The same virtues that led Jesus to the cross are the same virtues that are needed in us, allowing the cross to live in us. There is something about walking in humility and meekness that creates pathways for this power to live in us.

So how is this done practically? I think back to Jesus talking to Peter when He said that if someone wishes to come after Him, he must take up HIS cross, meaning the path that God has for him. Peter's cross was to lay aside his selfish ambitions, his personnel dreams, and to follow Jesus. This may take different paths for different people. The self-life will always pop up and want to put itself forward. Peter's self-life wanted to exalt itself and find a way to get the position he wanted. The ironic thing is that Jesus wanted the same thing for Peter, but how that was going to be accomplished was much different. This is where true faith in God is tested. Peter was tested in the time of his trial after Jesus died and his whole world came crashing down. Jesus told Peter that Satan desired to sift him as wheat (Luke 22:31); which meant that at Peter's lowest point of disappointment, Satan was going to tempt him to get angry at God and turn to the world for comfort.

Peter's mind had to be tumbling. Everything he hoped for and everything they had worked for came tumbling down in a moment of time. Despair, fear, doubt, and accusation were going off in his mind like firecrackers in succession. Peter must have kept going over internally what he boasted about and the reality of what happened. He went down the path of dying to self.

Jesus arose from the dead and appeared to His disciples. He confronted Peter with the question, "Do you love me more than all your fellow brethren?" The knife just cut open the flesh again so all natural life could bleed out. Peter admitted that he did not love Jesus more than the others. He was completely humiliated and broken. Then Jesus breathed new life in him and said, "Go feed My sheep." He was ready to start walking in the kingdom authority that was ordained for him to walk in. He lost his life, and God breathed into him His life, His ways, and His path.

# REVELATIONS OF THE WORK OF THE CROSS

The cross of Calvary and the death of Jesus the Christ was the holiest act of all history. Holiest because it was the most transcendent in its measurement of everything it did and accomplished. The work of Calvary was transcendent in the mercy it exhibited, love it demonstrated, kindness it displayed, grace it bestowed, goodness it proved, wisdom it revealed, power it released, authority it gave, riches it conferred, strength it imparted, glory it showed, honor it granted, and blessing it brought to mankind.

One day while fellowshipping with the Lord and meditating on the cross, the Lord told me that all of heaven centers on the cross. If heaven centers on the cross, then earth does also. Later one day, I was reading a book by Rebecca Springer. She had an experience where she had died and went to heaven and wrote what she saw heaven. In her testimony, all of heaven centered on the cross. I almost jumped out my body when I read that!

The cross is the path of humility and meekness. Jesus humbled himself and shed His glory to do the will of the Father. He came to earth to bring to man what He could not bring on himself, which was salvation, forgiveness of sins and brings us back into a sonship relationship with God When the same mind that is in Christ is also in us, the same forces and powers that are released through the work of the cross are released in us.

The cross was not given just for the forgiveness of man's sins. The forgiveness of sins needed to bring about the ultimate purpose, which was to redeem mankind so we can experience the purpose of our existence. This purpose is to dwell in God, and God to dwell in him. The cross brought a unity between man and God, where we could live in Him and He in us. It is the duality of existence of God in man and man in God.

I want to illustrate how the power of the cross works in us through some other revelations of the cross that the Lord gave me. We understand from the scriptures that when Jesus rose from the dead, He did not have a flesh-and-blood body anymore. He has a flesh-and-bone body (Luke 24:39). When Jesus died on the cross His natural blood spilled out and was taken to the mercy seat of heaven as an offering to take away the sins of man once and for all.

Our natural life is in the blood. It does so many things to keep us alive. The blood is the medium that brings life-giving oxygen to the muscles in our body, which allow them to operate. The blood goes through our lungs and exchanges carbon dioxide for oxygen. Carbon dioxide is the waste product in our respiratory cycle. The blood also operates with our digestive system and brings all the nutrients we need to allow the body to function normally. It acts as the medium of transportation to bring all the toxins that build up in our body to be filtered and expelled from the body.

When Jesus rose from the dead, He did not have natural blood flowing in His flesh-and-bone body. He had the spiritual blood of heaven, which was the glory of God. Paul tells us that Jesus was raised from the dead by the glory of the Father (Romans 6:4). Jesus said that He came to give us His glory when we are in union with Jesus through the power of the cross. The power of that cross works in us. At the new birth, God recreates our spirit in the image and likeness of Him and places in us a new heart. This new heart pumps that glory through us.

Just as the natural heart pumps blood through our body to allow us to live, the spiritual heart pumps the glory of God in our spiritual man. As this happens, it gives us all things that pertain to life and godliness; it cleanses us and transforms us into the image and likeness of God. I find it interesting in Matthew 16 that after Peter makes his great confession of the revelation—Jesus as the Christ—he is rebuked and exhorted to give up his life so that God's life could live in him. The next story recorded in the Bible says that exactly six days after this rebuke, Jesus was transfigured on the mountain in all His glory before Peter, James, and John. Considering the timing, Jesus was giving them a foretaste of what was going to happen in them through the work of the cross. As they continued walking the path in meekness and humility, they were going to receive the authority of the Lion in the kingdom.

# PART 5: KINGDOM MASTER BUILDERS OF THE BIBLE

# MOSES, THE MEEKEST OF ALL

I would like to end this book with examples of the greatest of leaders in the kingdom. The easiest one to talk about is Jesus the Christ, who shed the glory of the Father and became man. He refused the glory that man wanted to give Him, and submitted to the will of the Father. He demonstrated the perfection of meekness and humility in bodily form and went to the cross. Wherefore God highly exalted Him and gave Him the name above all names that at the name of Jesus every knee will bow, and every tongue will confess that Jesus is Lord. He is the One who is worthy to open, read, and look at the scroll that releases the greatest judgments on earth. He is the One who the angels announced as the "Root of David" and "The Lion of the Tribe of Judah."

When John went to look at the throne and saw this royal person, He saw the Lamb that was slain with all royalty and honor encapsulated in Him. He is the One in heaven who the angels and elders sing about. He is the One who is worthy to receive power, riches, wisdom, strength, honor, glory, and blessing. He is the One in heaven of whom every creature in heaven, and on the earth, and under the earth, and under the sea are saying, "Blessing, honor, glory, and power be unto Him who sits on the throne and the Lamb forever." I don't think I need to go any further about Jesus. So let's look at some other men of God.

If I were to look in the Bible and guess who had the most profound spiritual impact on our Judeo-Christian heritage, it would have to be Moses, King David, and Paul. Let's spend some time discussing each of them.

Moses was born to a Hebrew woman during a time of great oppression from Pharaoh. Being concerned for her child's safety, she put him in a basket and set it afloat in the river Nile. He was then taken by Pharaoh's daughter and raised in Pharaoh's house for forty years. In Acts 7:22-23, Stephen preached that Moses was highly educated in all learnings of Egypt and was a man of power in word and deed. At the age of forty, Moses wanted to visit his brethren. The scriptures don't tell us how Moses knew the Jews were his brethren. Moses must have felt the call from God to do something to deliver his brethren. As many young people who feel the call of God, he did too, and started pursuing that calling through his plans and the ways of man. He killed an Egyptian soldier who was mistreating one of his brethren. Then the next day he went to his brethren again and tried to settle a dispute. When one of the men who was involved in the dispute identified Moses as the one who killed the Egyptian, Moses fled for fear of his life.

Moses went out thinking that he was going to deliver his brethren. But he ended up running for his life. He needed to get to the other side of the desert and meet God. He needed to get stripped of his ways, his thoughts, and his opinions on how this was going to be done. He spent forty years being a shepherd on the other side of the desert. One day Moses ran into God on Mount Horeb through a bush that was blazing with fire but was not consumed. Then God started to talk to Moses from the burning bush and told him that He wanted to deliver His people from Egypt, and that He was going to use Moses as the instrument to do it. Moses was asking God as to how he was going to do this, and what he should do if they didn't believe him.

> Then Moses said to the LORD, "Please, Lord, I have never been eloquent, neither recently nor in time past, nor since you have spoken to your servant; for I am slow of speech and slow of tongue."

## MOSES, THE MEEKEST OF ALL

> The LORD said to him, "Who has made man's mouth? Or who makes him mute or deaf, or seeing or blind? Is it not I, the LORD? "Now then go, and I, even I, will be with your mouth, and teach you what you are to say." But he said, "Please, Lord, now send the message by whomever you will."
>
> Then the anger of the LORD burned against Moses, and He said, "Is there not your brother Aaron the Levite? I know that he speaks fluently. And moreover, behold, he is coming out to meet you; when he sees you, he will be glad in his heart (Exodus 4:10-14).

Moses was an eloquent man while in Egypt, according to Stephen's account in Acts. After Moses lived in the desert for so many years as a shepherd, he called himself a stutterer. Moses went so far to say that he was always slow in speech. So who was telling the truth? I think they both were. Moses got to a place where he had lost all of his dreams, strength, and confidence in himself and in God, and what he perceived as God's calling for his life. I guess living in the desert for forty years doesn't produce a lot of hope, and it didn't seem like anything was going to change anytime soon. Moses was at the point where all hope of what he thought he was supposed to do was gone. Then God came! He breathed His true plan and strategy of how these things were to be carried out. Most importantly, this started an interaction and relationship with God that few probably ever had.

Think of the things that Moses experienced with God. He was with God for forty days and forty nights—not once, but twice. The first time he sat in the presence of God for six days before he or God spoke to each other. What was going on? Imagine just sitting for six days and looking at someone and not saying anything… Most people would say that it was boring. When you are in the presence of the living, holy, and beautiful God, you just get captivated by who He is—and it never gets old! As we read in Revelation 4, that is why when the creatures stand in the presence of God, they continually cry "holy." They only cry in response to something they see about God's character and nature that they have not seen before. It never stops; it goes on and on. I believe Moses was beholding the same holiness and beauty of the Lord and was captivated by who he was interacting with. What happens to us in that situation? We are changed by the glory of the Lord. God does something on the inside of us. Our spiritual heart melts and we become transformed into a union with Him.

After Moses waited for six days, God spoke to him on the seventh day. I believe this is an important pattern. Beholding God softens our heart and then He speaks with the sword from His mouth and writes it on our heart, which is the womb of the spirit.

The second time Moses was with God for forty days and forty nights, it was proceeded by Moses asking God to show him His glory as he interceded for the children of Israel, asking for the presence of the Lord to go with them as he led them to the Promised Land. This happened after the sin of the golden calf. Moses went into God's presence. God made His glory pass by Moses, and there Moses proclaimed the goodness, mercy, and loving-kindness of God. Because the presence was so holy, Moses understood that it was God's judgment. But this was only after he saw the goodness of God. God desires to show us His goodness before any form of judgment.

When Moses came out after being with God the second time, the children of Israel could not look at Moses' face, because it was reflecting the glory of God. Moses had to cover his face when he talked to the children of Israel. Moses was being transformed by the presence of the Lord. These continued experiences with God caused Moses to go lower and lower with God. The lower and more reduced you are, the more God lifts you up to dwell continually in His presence.

In Numbers 12, Moses recalls an incident where Miriam and Aaron were speaking against him. They were jealous of the way God spoke with Moses. They tried to discredit him using the fact that he had a wife who wasn't of Jewish decent. She was an Ethiopian. Moses did not try to defend Himself. God defended Him. This is a perfect example of selfish ambition, a religious manipulative spirit entering in. They tried to take a perceived fault of Moses and turn it into something it was not, in order to gain more recognition and authority.

> While they were at Hazeroth, Miriam and Aaron criticized Moses because he had married a Cushite woman. They said, "Has the Lord spoken only through Moses? Hasn't he spoken through us, too?" But the Lord heard them. (Now Moses was very humble—more humble than any other person on earth) (Numbers 12:1-3 NLT).

God defended Moses and judged Miriam and Aaron. I want to draw your attention to the source of Moses' authority. He was humbler (meeker) than any other person on the earth. Moses wrote this about himself, this is what happens when you learn to live and enjoy His presence. It was recorded in the Beatitudes many years later as, "Blessed are the meek for they shall inherit the earth."

Moses learned the secret to walking in the true authority and power that God had ordained him to walk in. To this day, we see that the authority and revelation of his life and ministry were imparted to Judaism and then passed on through the new covenant to Christianity. Moses' effect on his era, as well as future eras is profound. It came from learning to walk in the meekness and humility of the Lamb.

# THE APOSTLE PAUL: THE WORST SINNER & LEAST APOSTLE

In most Christian denominations, of all the apostles, Paul is probably the most highly thought of. He is considered as an example of a Christian missionary. When you read through the book of Acts you will see how much he endured in his ministry by the hands of the Gentiles, the Jews, the Jewish believers in Christ, and even the Christian church. One must marvel at what he accomplished. We can get even more personnel insight into Paul as we read through 1 and 2 Corinthians. These are his most personal letters where he defends his calling and ministry before the Corinthian church.

In the latter part of the book of Acts, we see that Paul was staying in his own quarters in Rome when he was taken to be judged by the Roman courts. He made one more final defense in front of the Jews in Rome and was expecting that negative information was going to be passed on to them from Jerusalem. However, nothing was sent. Paul made an all-day defense of preaching of Jesus as the Christ. There was some great dispute among the hearers. During the last years of his ministry and life, Paul was abandoned by most of his disciples, and he just preached to anyone who came to him. Probably many people in his day may have thought that his ministry came to a crash and that he had very little influence left. Today we see that the writings of Paul have the most profound effect on the Christian church; he wrote two thirds of the canonized New Testament text. Let's look at some of Paul's writings and figure out the authority he walked in.

The first characteristic is to not think more highly of ourselves than we should and recognize that we are what we are by the grace of God.

Let's look at three scriptures from Paul's writings:

> It is a trustworthy statement, deserving full acceptance, that Christ Jesus came into the world to save sinners, **among whom I am foremost of all.** Yet for this reason I found mercy, so that in me as the foremost, Jesus Christ might demonstrate His perfect patience as an example for those who would believe in Him for eternal life (1 Timothy 1:15-16).

> For I am the least of the apostles, and not fit to be called an apostle, because I persecuted the church of God. But by the grace of God I am what I am, and His grace toward me did not prove vain; but I labored even more than all of them, yet not I, but the grace of God with me (1 Corinthians 15:9-10).

> To me, the very least of all saints, this grace was given, to preach to the Gentiles the unfathomable riches of Christ (Ephesian 3:8).

Let's think about this: Who wrote these words? The Apostle Paul! What made him think that he was a complete work of the grace of God? Paul penned the words, "He made him who knew no sin to be sin on our behalf, so that we might become the righteousness of God in Him" (2 Corinthians 5:21). Paul knew who he was in Christ. He knew that he was a new creature. He knew that he was crucified, died, buried, quickened, resurrected, and seated in the heavenlies through Christ's substitutionary work of the cross. With the knowledge of these truths comes a sober understanding that it was only the work of God that can do what it did in Paul's life. Paul penned that we are saved by grace through faith; it is not of ourselves, but the gift of God that no man could boast (Ephesians 2:8). He counted himself the greatest of all sinners. This is not a bad confession, but it is a sober understanding of the work of God that was accomplished in Him. He knew that he was a picture-perfect demonstration of the patience and mercy of God; the redemptive power of God to create a brand-new person.

Paul defended his ministry because of his great calling, but he knew that his ministry and his conversion was an act of great mercy and grace that was imparted to him from the Father above. I like to call Paul "The Apostle of Great Grace." He said that he was the least of the apostles because he persecuted the church of God. We don't know how many people Paul had thrown in prison or killed. It was a well-known fact in the church as to what Paul was doing. It is safe to assume that it was enough that he had to have run into the families of those who he may have harmed during his pre-conversion days. Therefore, he was constantly confronted with his pre-conversion days. He knew that he had received mercy because of his ignorant acts. No wonder he was the one who said that if any man be in Christ, he is a new creature; a totally new being. He knew that when God said, "Let there be light" and created the world, He was also saying, "Let there be light in Paul," and the light of the beautiful knowledge of the Son of God shown upon Paul.

This constant reminder worked within him a great appreciation for God's mercy and grace. He said that though he was the least of the apostles, the grace of God worked in him more than anyone else. He noted that he labored in God more than all the others, not himself, but the grace of God. God is willing to use His ability on our behalf to bring on us what we cannot bring on ourselves—even though we don't deserve it. Grace works through humility; Humility brings you to a place of nothingness in self and awareness that God is everything. It reduces your own estimation of your ability and knowledge and understanding.

Therefore, Paul went on to explain to the Philippian church that everything of worldly gain to him, he counted as nothing, worthless, not more valuable than a pile of waste. He knew that the knowledge of God was more important. He wanted to know Him, the power that was in His resurrection and the communion of His suffering so he may be made in complete conformity to His death, that he may attain the full outflowing of the resurrection power of God. He knew that the lower he would go, the higher he could go. That is why we should press on towards the high calling of God in Christ Jesus. The high calling is the low calling. Jesus said, "He who humbles himself will be exalted." To be exalted means to be at the highest place of opulence and prosperity.

> For thus says the high and exalted One, who lives forever, whose name is Holy, "I dwell on a high and holy place, And also with the contrite and lowly of spirit In order to revive the spirit of the lowly and to revive the heart of the contrite (Isaiah 57:15).

Paul lived this out in his relationship with Jesus. He learned how to dwell within the high and holy place. When you dwell there, you become aware of the complete desolation of man who is apart from Christ and the sin that lives in the old man. That is why Paul said that he was the least of not only the apostles, but the least of the saints, and the greatest of sinners. It wasn't a bad confession, but a statement of living fact apart from the grace of God. He came to a place of contrition before God. *Contrition* means to be reduced to nothing. God does not reduce us to nothing in order to belittle and shame us into submission to Him; He reduces us by the revelation of Himself. What that does is open us to a work of love and grace that only a holy and good God could do. He reduces our self-will and self-assertion and builds up a spiritual life. He imparts the knowledge of who and what we have been made to be, and reveals the place and purpose we have before Him that does not bring pride or self-exaltation. It is the place where the Lion could assert His authority through the meekness of the Lamb.

The second characteristic that led to Paul's authority is he understood that God was the One who examined his motives and that he would be accountable for them at the judgment seat of Christ. Let's explore some other statements Paul made in his second letter to the Corinthian church.

# THE APOSTLE PAUL: THE WORST SINNER & LEAST APOSTLE

This is the most personal of Paul's letters. They were questioning his apostleship and spiritual authority. Throughout the letter, Paul described the true character and nature of his ministry. Paul's uses a word repeatedly in the letter. The word is about speaking and conducting himself in godly sincerity. The root of the word *sincerity* means to be pure or found pure when unfolded and examined by the suns brightest light. Paul understood the judgment seat of Christ. He said that the motives of men's hearts would be exposed, and that we would receive rewards for what we have done in the body, whether good or bad (evil). He knew that there is nothing hidden from God, and that His magnificent light, character, and nature would expose all things that are not in accordance with His nature and being.

The third characteristic is that Paul's desire was not to draw people to himself, but to draw people to Christ. This sounds like a simple and true statement that most would agree with. When notoriety is gained, as a leader it is very easy to draw people to ourselves rather than to God. When the Corinthians were dividing themselves up saying, "I am of Paul," or "I am of Apollos," or "I am of Cephas (Peter)," Paul wrote to them to remind them that they are just servants and messengers of God with a role to fulfill, but God is the one who causes the increase. He implored them to stop dividing themselves into groups (denominations) and receive the grace given by each of His servants and allow that to minister and cause growth in the things of God.

God communicates with His people through spiritual experiences. Many times these are supernatural experiences. I have heard many ministers talk about dreams, visions, healings, miracles, signs, and wonders. Hearing them encourages us to walk with God. I do believe that God gives us those things to share. Please notice something Paul said to the Corinthian church while explaining his ministry in 2 Corinthians 12. He was sharing that he, too, could glory in his dreams, visions, and spiritual experiences. He revealed that he was caught up to the third heaven and saw things that he could not even speak of. His point was that he didn't want to boast about those things as a mark and confirmation of his ministry or spirituality. He said that he wanted to boast of his weakness and frailties, knowing that in his weakness God made him strong. He also said that he did not want to boast about those things. He didn't want people to think more of him than they saw and heard in him. Paul was more concerned about people seeing the works of God in his behavior and actions rather than just hearing his spiritual experiences. Too often, we get enamored with someone's spiritual experiences and think that it is a mark of their superior spirituality. It is often just the grace of God working through them for His good pleasure. We need to be more concerned with godly character, love, and behavior. These activities reveal the true spirituality of a person. Before we start sharing any of these things, we should take a step back and ask God if we should be sharing our spiritual experiences. Perhaps we should just ponder about them for a while, allowing God to do the work that is needed in us spiritually, then we can carry our experiences in perspective to the bigger picture of our spiritual growth.

Paul shares that because of these revelations, a messenger of Satan was sent to harass him. The word *messenger* means angel. A fallen angel of Satan was sent to harass him. The question is: What was this messenger doing? As I read through the New Testament and looked at Paul's life, he was constantly getting harassed by the Jews, Gentiles, and others for his testimony and preaching. As he traveled from town to town, the Jews or some other groups would stir the crowd around Paul and persecute him. This persecution took on many forms. He was whipped by the Jews five times (each time with forty lashes), beaten three times with rods, stoned once, and shipwrecked three times.

I wonder how many times Paul thought he was going to die, either from the pain or the amount of persecution. He asked the Lord to take this away. God told him that His grace was more than anything Paul needed and that it would sustain him. He learned that if he would embrace his weakness, God would empower him with grace. Remember, God's grace is His willingness to use His power on our behalf to bring on us what we cannot bring on ourselves even though we don't deserve it. Paul humbled himself before God and God gave him grace to be humble. Because Paul also said that God's grace worked with him more than anyone else, we can conclude that Paul had humbled himself more than anyone else. He learned the secret of how to dwell with God and how to maintain his spiritual vitality and passion through the midst of the direst of circumstances.

Paul's letters to the churches are full of references to meekness and humility. In Ephesians 4:2, he exhorts the Ephesian church to be humble, meek, and patient with one another, giving allowance for other faults, and to walk in love so that they can stay in unity. In Galatians 6:1, he exhorts the Galatian church to have a spirit of meekness with one another when one had a fault and was trying to work towards restoration, understanding that the same fault or problem could overtake another also. In Colossians 3:12, he exhorted the Colossian church to clothe themselves with tender mercy, kindness, humility, gentleness, and patience, making allowance for others' faults and forgiving them. Making allowance for others' faults is not just ignoring them. It is seeing them as God sees them, and not just identifying them by their faults. He says we are to be patient in correction, leading people by word and example towards Christ, the One who can change and transform them.

Paul wrote that we are to speak the truth in love, and by that, we would grow up to the fullest measure that God wanted the body of Christ to grow into. When we speak the truth out of anger, jealousy, and strife, it will not accomplish what is needed, nor correct and restore. Sometimes we correct others just because we want to belittle and control someone, but our correction needs to come from a place where restoration and growth needs to happen, not destruction and despair from the severity of the correction. Paul was always correcting the church, but you can see through his writings that his motivation was to build up and restore so they could reach the fullness of what God wanted for them.

This kind of mindset and understanding does not innately come to anyone. This comes from a place of ongoing spiritual maturity and growth. I'm sure Paul had his faults and shortcomings, as we all do. I'm sure that he had his internal battles of just wanting to blast some people, going up one side of them and down the other for what they were doing to him. However, Paul kept moving forward to the place with God where he was transformed and changed to His image. Thereby his actions and life would be indicative of what he knew by experience. He learned by reason and constant interaction with God. He learned how to have his spiritual senses trained to discern what was evil, self-serving, and vindictive and what was good, edifying, and serving common good.

The secret to Paul's authority, which has had long lasting effects in the kingdom, is that he learned how to walk in the meekness of the Lamb, so that he could receive the authority of the Lion.

# KING DAVID, THE SWEET PSALMIST OF ISRAEL

Let's talk about King David, who God called "a man after His own heart." He was a king, a priest, a prophet, and as David called himself "the sweet psalmist of Israel." He led Israel during one of its most glorious times. He was a man who had many great victories and experiences with God, but also a man who had many failures. He exhibited many great attributes as a leader and had some great examples of how human weakness and frailty can corrupt our leadership and lessen the authority given to us. He exhibited great humility, faith, and patience, but also showed insecurity in weakness—especially after his leadership was established. We can see that the humility and meekness he exhibited was what propelled him into a place of leadership. We can also see that the loss of humility and meekness, which is pride in action, was the source of his failures and faults.

Among all the kings of Israel, David's history is written about the most. God rejected Saul from being the king of Israel. Samuel the prophet was in mourning because God had rejected Saul. God came to him one day and told him to stop mourning, and to get up and go and anoint a son of Jesse in the city of Bethlehem as the king of Israel. Samuel obeys and there he meets Jesse and his sons. Upon meeting each one of them, he pondered based on their appearance as to which one was the anointed of the Lord. But none of them were. Then Samuel asked Jesse if they were all his sons. Jesse replied that there was one more—the youngest one. Not only did Samuel judge the sons based on their outward appearance, but so did Jesse. God told him not to judge people by their outward appearance, but to judge like He does—look at people's hearts. Samuel looked at seven of Jesse's sons, and none of them were chosen by God to be the king of Israel. Then Jesse sends for David who was out tending the flocks in the field. As David approached, the Lord spoke to Samuel and told him that David was the one. Samuel anointed David, and the Spirit of the Lord came upon him, and the favor of the Lord followed him in all that he did.

God had rejected Saul from being king. Saul was trying to maintain control over the kingdom. Without the anointing or the hand of the Lord present with him, he was treading water at best. When you don't have God's anointing or His hand in what you are doing, you need to rely on the wisdom and understanding of the world and men. Saul was in a place without God's hand guiding him, and an evil spirit was harassing him. He never learned how to establish his own relationship with the Lord so he relied on his own understanding. James writes in his letter saying that we must submit to God and resist the devil, and he will flee from us. Saul had very little submission to God, so the harassment of the evil spirit sent him into deep internal conflict and depression.

David appears on the scene, anointed of the Lord. One of Saul's advisors heard that David was a skilled musician and that the hand of the Lord was with him. Saul invited David into his house to minister to him musically to bring him peace. Notice what is written about David in 1 Samuel 16:18 (KJV):

> Then answered one of the servants, and said, Behold, I have seen a son of Jesse the Beth-lehemite, that is cunning in playing, and a mighty valiant man, and a man of war, and prudent in matters, and a comely person, and the LORD is with him.

I am not sure where this servant of Saul got all this information regarding David from. The only thing that is recorded about David is that he was the youngest of Jesse's sons and that he tended the sheep. In the next chapter, we read about the battle between the Philistines and Goliath. David was not even called to go to war with his older brothers. Maybe this servant had insight to things not even revealed yet, because it was not long after that that all the things that he said came to pass. It is said that David loved Saul greatly. When David came before Saul and played his harp, the evil spirit would leave Saul.

As we continue along in the chapter, we read that David slayed Goliath. David was taken into Saul's house, and there Jonathan, Saul's oldest son, made a covenant with David and they became like brothers. David was a part of Saul's men of war and he prospered wherever he went. Then something happened that changed this perfectly happy-scene. As they were coming back from war with the Philistines, the women of the city were singing and dancing, saying Saul had slain his thousands and David his tens of thousands. Once Saul heard that, he became suspicious and jealous of David.

Many times, leaders will recognize the presence of the Lord on a young person and bring them into their fold. The question is whether they just bring them in to use their gift to further their kingdom (or ministry), or do they bring them in to train them so the kingdom can be advanced for everyone's benefit. Insecurity in leadership will bring out all kinds of evil against those whom the leaders are threatened by. They will pick on every fault, amplify every perceived failure, and use anything to gain advantage over their perceived rival. The problem with this behavior is that it just takes away from the real authority that has been given to them. It is the opposite of the humility of the Lamb; it is like a lion seeking whom he may devour.

From that time onward, Saul plotted to destroy and discredit David. He tried to get him killed in battle; he even tried to kill him himself. David had to flee and live on the run, even though he was the anointed of the Lord, the king whom God wanted.

David, like most young leaders who are persecuted by those they serve under, was perplexed. Why was Saul doing this? He was questioning if there was something he did wrong. Jonathan consoled David and told him that it was nothing he did, rather it was the jealousy and evil of his father.

David was on the run, and Saul and his men were seeking him all around the nation of Israel. We read in 1 Samuel 22 that Saul's jealousy had driven him so insane that he killed eighty-five priests of the Lord. This jealously caused so much strife and dissension in the house of Saul and throughout Judah and Israel.

Now during this time of Saul pursuing David, Saul came close to finding David twice. David could have killed Saul both of those times. I want to point out something significant about the character of David that allowed him to attain the authority he was destined for. Each time, David did not step out of the authority that God had given him. David knew that God anointed him as king, and he also knew that Saul was still king because God had not removed him. God rejected Saul from the future. We can know God's plan for our life and understand our purpose, but that doesn't mean that we pursue the plan and purpose in ways that God doesn't want us to.

Saul was pursing David and went into a cave to rest, not knowing that David and his men were hiding in the farthest recesses of that cave. Immediately, David's men assumed that it was God who delivered Saul to them and that David should kill him—and he would be justified in doing so. David could not do it; instead, he cut a piece off of Saul's coat. Even with that, his heart condemned him, and he felt that he was disrespecting God and His anointed.

David called out to Saul and told him what happened in the cave. Saul saw David's kindness and wept. Saul was so distraught that he even admitted that David would be king. However, Saul was so deceived and confused, his ambition and pride completely blinded him and soon started pursuing David again. We read this in 1 Samuel 26.

The point I want to make here is that just because you are called and anointed, and just because you may have been wronged by someone who is jealous of you, it doesn't change the principle that judgment is in the hand of the Lord. In His time, He will put you in a place of authority and take another down. When we start taking judgment ourselves, we go down a slippery path of pride and self-righteousness. We start thinking that we are more important than we are. This will lead us down the same path of deception that Saul went into.

Shortly after that event in the cave, Saul and his son Jonathan died in the battle against the Philistines. When David found out, he did not rejoice because he could stop running and become king. Rather, he lamented over Saul and Jonathan. The same grace that made David king, also taught him about the mercy and kindness of the Lord. David loved Saul so much that he lamented in 2 Samuel 1:19:

> The beauty of Israel is slain upon thy high places: How are the mighty fallen!

It took about fourteen years after Samuel prophesied over David that he would become king, until the time when David received the first portion of the kingdom. David did not just go up and take the place of king. Instead, he inquired of the Lord, and the Lord told him to go up to Judah where the men of Judah would anoint him as king of Judah. Then it was seven years and six months later before David would be anointed as the king of Israel and completely unite the land. So it took over twenty-one years before the word of God was fulfilled.

Let's look at some other characteristics of David's authority and leadership. David realized that his anointing and leadership was not for his benefit, but for the benefit of the people.

> So David made the fortress his home, and he called it the City of David. He extended the city, starting at the supporting terraces and working inward. And David became more and more powerful, because the Lord God of heaven's Armies was with him….And David realized that the Lord had confirmed him as king over Israel and

had blessed his kingdom for the sake of his people Israel (2 Samuel 5:9-10, 12 NLT).

So, David reigned over all Israel; and David administered justice and righteousness for all his people (2 Samuel 8:15).

And David realized that the LORD had established him as king over Israel, and that his kingdom was highly exalted, for the sake of His people Israel (1 Chronicles 14:2).

It's easy to take authority to yourself and use positional authority completely for your own benefit. Humility recognizes that the position is for the benefit of all, and not just the one in position. Peter so clearly stated it in 1 Peter 5:1-5, that leaders were to feed the flock of God, not force them into obedience or lord over them; not just for money, but willingly help and pastor them by being examples to them. Again, this is a characteristic of a leading lion that walks in the humility of the Lamb.

David understood that what he was given was for the benefit of the people. The kingdom advanced for the benefit of the people, and David was to administer justice and righteousness. These are all kingdom principles which allow God-given kingdom authority to grow.

David loved God, and it was more important to him to worship the Lord and acknowledge His lordship than it was to appear as distinguished before people. When David finally got the ark of the covenant back, which represented the presence of God, he was so overjoyed that he danced before the Lord.

> Then King David was told, "The LORD has blessed Obed-edom's household and everything he has because of the Ark of God." So David went there and brought the Ark of God from the house of Obed-edom to the City of David with a great celebration. After the men who were carrying the Ark of the LORD had gone six steps, David sacrificed a bull and a fattened calf. And David danced before the LORD with all his might, wearing a priestly garment. So

# KING DAVID, THE SWEET PSALMIST OF ISRAEL

> David and all the people of Israel brought up the Ark of the LORD with shouts of joy and the blowing of rams' horns.
>
> David retorted to Michal, "I was dancing before the LORD, who chose me above your father and all his family! He appointed me as the leader of Israel, the people of the LORD, so I celebrate before the LORD. Yes and I am willing to look even more foolish than this, even to be humiliated in my own eyes! But those servant girls you mentioned will indeed think I am distinguished!" So Michal, the daughter of Saul, remained childless throughout her entire life (2 Samuel 6:12-15, 21-23 NLT).

Not only did David worship God and dance before Him as he brought the ark back to Jerusalem, but David created a tent of worship for the Lord and did something that was never established before. He took the Levites, the singers, and the musicians, and established twenty-four hours of prayer and worship.

> He appointed some of the Levites as ministers before the ark of the Lord, even to celebrate and to thank and praise the Lord God of Israel: Asaph the chief, and second to him Zechariah, then Jeiel, Shemiramoth, Jehiel, Mattithiah, Eliab, Benaiah, Obed-edom and Jeiel, with musical instruments, harps, lyres; also Asaph played loud-sounding cymbals, and Benaiah and Jahaziel the priests blew trumpets continually before the ark of the covenant of God. Then on that day David first assigned Asaph and his relatives to give thanks to the Lord (1 Chronicles 16:4-7).
>
> So he left Asaph and his relatives there **before the ark of the covenant of the Lord to minister before the ark continually**, as every day's work required; and Obed-edom with his 68 relatives; Obed-edom, also the son of Jeduthun, and Hosah as gatekeepers (1 Chronicles 16:37-38).

> And 4,000 were gatekeepers, and 4,000 were praising the Lord with the instruments which David made for giving praise. David divided them into divisions according to the sons of Levi: Gershon, Kohath, and Merari (1 Chronicles 23:5-6).
>
> Moreover, David and the commanders of the army set apart for the service some of the sons of Asaph and of Heman and of Jeduthun, who were to prophesy with lyres, harps and cymbals; and the number of those who performed their service was: (inspired prophetic psalms)…Their number who were trained in singing to the Lord, with their relatives, all who were skillful, was 288 (1 Chronicles 25:1, 7).

Not only did David appoint this worship in the temple, but he participated in it. Today the book of Psalms is referred as the song book of Israel. Most of the Psalms were written during this time, and they came out of inspired utterance as they worshipped God and sang before Him in their continuous times of worship and prayer.

David was known for many things. He was known for killing Goliath, a great warrior, a great king, he united Judah and Israel, and established a great earthly kingdom for Israel. The primary thing David should have been known for is that he was a worshipper of God. He was also a great songwriter, inspired by words from God. Let's look at what David said about himself at the end of his life:

> Now these are the last words of David. David the son of Jesse declares, the man who was raised on high declares, the anointed of the God of Jacob, **and the sweet psalmist of Israel, "The Spirit of the Lord spoke by me, And His word was on my tongue"** (2 Samuel 23:1-2).

One translation says that he was the most popular songwriter in Israel, the sweet psalmist. In Psalm 27:4, David reveals his heart by saying that the one thing he desired and sought after was to dwell in the house of the Lord and behold the beauty of the Lord and mediate on Him. That is what David did. I think his times of worship were well known, and people probably wanted to be there when he worshipped and sang. He was the most popular songwriter in all of Israel. When David worshipped, God showed forth His glory. I can imagine how this time was a great spiritual renaissance where God's presence and anointing was so strong. We can refer to this in our modern vernacular—Revival!

It is a common belief that there are mansions in heaven for all inhabitants. Most people base this on John 14:2. I think a better translation is, "In my Father's house there are many dwelling places." Jesus goes on to explain about us abiding in Him and Him abiding in us. The words *abide* and *dwell* are essentially the same word. What Jesus was talking about was "man dwelling in God and God dwelling in us." Because of the work of the cross, we know that God does not dwell in earthen temples made by man, but by spiritual temples made by God. We are the temple of God now. Jesus also spoke about how His Father's house shall be called a house of prayer. Therefore, our house must be a house of prayer.

So our house—our temple—should be a house of prayer. We need to build our temple of worship and fellowship with God so that He may reveal Himself to us and transform us; we become what we behold.

Jesus also prayed that His kingdom would come, and His will would be done on earth as it is in heaven. Our bodies are made of earth. For the kingdom to come, the dominion of God on earth must happen in our earthen temple. We do this by cultivating our temple as a dwelling place of God.

The reason I am going down this path is that this practice of continual worship and prayer will guide us toward continual meekness and humility before God. His presence will continually transform us, change us, and humble us. This will lead to greater authority. Remember that the authority of the Lion rests in the meekness of the Lamb. Losing your passion for His presence and allowing complacency to grow its roots in your life will certainly allow a greater opportunity for sin and failure to happen. We see this happen in David's life. This led to problems in the kingdom and people questioning his authority and leadership.

There is not a lot said about David's sin with Bathsheba, but it does say that when the kings went out to war, David did not go out and do what was customary for kings. Likewise, when we are not doing what we are supposed to be doing, we will find ourselves doing things that we should not be doing. I think David got to a point where he was comfortable. He was the king of Judah, he was king of Israel, and he was winning battles, obtaining wealth, and shoring up his position of leadership in the land. All the things that God had promised him seemed to have come to pass. These are the times when it is easy to stop doing the things that allowed us to get to the position we are currently in. As we look at David's life, we see that he worshipped and prayed. He was a warrior of the kingdom, he administered justice for all kingdoms for the benefit of the people, and he was the sweet psalmist of Israel (most popular songwriter in all of Israel). He worshipped continually before the Lord, dwelling in His presence, and beholding the beauty of the Lord.

This reminds me of Moses warning the people of Israel in Deuteronomy. He warned that once people dwell in nice houses, have eaten and are full, and have enough wealth, they should not become proud and forget that it was their God who gave them this ability to establish wealth and power in order to establish their covenant with Him. Pride is an evil disease that creeps up behind you before you know it. It motivates or inspires you to do things out of your own self-confidence. It results in failures and faults.

Let's recap what happened with David. One night he sees Bathsheba from the roof of the palace and desires her. It must be assumed that Bathsheba's house wasn't too far from David's in order for him to see her clearly. He pre-determines in his heart that he wants her and plans to get her to the palace. She obviously was a willing participant in the matter. David uses his position and authority for his own benefit. He has intercourse with her and commits adultery. She becomes pregnant. She was the wife of Uriah, one of David's thirty-seven mighty men. David probably had all these men live close to the palace because they were all faithful to him.

Once she became pregnant, David devised a plan for Uriah to come home during the battle to be with his wife, in order to cover up that David was the father of the child in her womb. But Uriah was so faithful to God, David, and his men, that he refused the pleasure of going home to be with his beautiful wife while his men were still in battle and the ark of the Lord was still dwelling in tents.

David had Uriah come in and tried to get him drunk so that he could get him to go down to his house to lay with his wife. However, Uriah does not. David then devises a plan to kill Uriah in battle. How wicked and evil is that! Once Uriah dies, then he can take Bathsheba as his own wife. He went from being a great king who administers justice to the people, to a premeditated murderer of one of his most faithful warriors.

Knowing the nature of man, I am sure whispers and rumors went through the city about what happened, especially among the faithful warriors who saw that one of their own was sent into an ambush to die. They were ordered to retreat and leave Uriah to fight and die on his own. It's no wonder that later on it was easy for Absalom, David's son, to steal the commitment of all of Israel away from David. He probably fed into the discontent that many had with the sinful actions of David. I will pick this up later in the chapter.

The sin is so great that Nathan the prophet is sent to publicly rebuke David. He reveals to David that he abused his authority, he did not administer justice, and he did things for his benefit, at the expense of others; which is the essential characteristic of evil. He was so deceived in his position and the blessings from God. He thought that he could supersede the law of God. Notice what David said after the prophet Nathan told him the story of the rich man taking advantage of the only possession of the poor man:

Then the LORD sent Nathan to David. And he came to him and said,

> "There were two men in one city, the one rich and the other poor. The rich man had a great many flocks and herds. But the poor man had nothing except one little ewe lamb which he bought and nourished; and it grew up together with him and his children. It would eat of his bread and drink of his cup and lie in his bosom, and was like a daughter to him. Now a traveler came to the rich man, and he was unwilling to take from his own flock or his own herd, to prepare for the wayfarer who had come to him; rather he took the poor man's ewe lamb and prepared it for the man who had come to him" (2 Samuel 12:1-4).

Then we see David's reaction and the rebuke of the Lord:

> Nathan then said to David, "You are the man! Thus says the LORD God of Israel, 'It is I who anointed you king over Israel and it is I who delivered you from the hand of Saul. I also gave you your master's house and your master's wives into your care, and I gave you the house of Israel and Judah; and if that had been too little, I would have added to you many more things like these! Why have you despised the word of the LORD by doing evil in His sight? You have struck down Uriah the Hittite with the sword, have taken his wife to be your wife, and have killed him with the sword of the sons of Ammon. Now therefore, the sword shall never depart from your house, because you have despised me and have taken the wife of Uriah the Hittite to be your wife.' Thus says the LORD, 'Behold, I will raise up evil against you from your own household; I will even take your wives before your eyes and give them to your companion, and he will lie with your wives in broad daylight. Indeed you did it secretly,

but I will do this thing before all Israel, and under the sun'" (2 Samuel 12:7-12).

From that day onward, calamity starts to befall David's household. First, the baby who Bathsheba gave birth to dies; Ammon rapes his sister, Tamar; Absalom, Tamar's brother, avenges the rape of his sister by having Ammon killed. Absalom is estranged from his father. Absalom starts to undermine his father's authority and starts to draw the heart of the people to him. Then he devises how to overthrow his father's kingship and become king. David had to flee Jerusalem for fear of being killed by Absalom. Absalom has intercourse with his father's wives and humiliates David, as foretold by Nathan. Then while trying to take control of the kingdom, a disaster befalls him—his beautiful hair, for which he was known, gets him caught on a tree, and he was killed by Joab, one of David's generals. David is totally grief-stricken, but then is restored as the king of Israel and Judah.

In conclusion, I want to go back to Revelation chapter 5, where the angel cried, "Who is worthy to open the seals?" John, by direction of the angel, looked at the throne and the one who the angel pointed out as worthy. He looked at the throne and he saw "a Lamb that had been slain," one who sacrificed Himself for the benefit of mankind, so the Father could have a loving family of kings and priests unto Himself, and fulfill the original commitment of God back in Exodus when the Jewish nation accepted God's invitation of betrothal.

The Lamb was to receive power. The Lamb was worthy of riches. The Lamb was worthy to receive might. The Lamb was worthy to receive honor. The Lamb was worthy to receive glory. The Lamb was worthy to receive blessing. The Lamb was worthy to receive dominion.

Jesus set the standard. We see that Moses, Paul, and David grabbed hold of this and were able to allow the authority of God to work through them.

My prayer for all who have read these words, is that the guiding principles that are written in this book will be written on your hearts as well. That the authority of the kingdom may be released in the world like never before, and Jesus' prayer will be answered, "Thy kingdom come, thy will be done on earth as it is in heaven."

# THE APOSTLE PETER—LEADER OF LEADERS

Yes! Kingdom Master Builder Peter! I have included him because he became a Master Builder. He was the principal figure in the first major outpouring of the Holy Spirit which started on the day of Pentecost. He was one of the principal leaders of the church and was a transitional leader to the second major outpouring of the Holy Spirit, which was the outpouring of the Holy Spirit to the Gentile nations. Remember Jesus told His disciples that they shall preach to Jerusalem, Judea, Samaria, and to the uttermost parts of the earth? In another words, They should start in Jerusalem, continue through the surrounding areas of the Jews—Judea, then to their related brothers in Samaria, and then to everyone else.

Reading the book of Acts, we see that the day of Pentecost and the launching of the Church Age started in Jerusalem, led by Peter through his first sermon when three thousand Jews recognized Jesus as the Messiah and received Him. Peter's second sermon was recoded in shortly thereafter in Acts 3, it is the story of Peter and John heading to the temple to prayer. Peter, led by the Holy Spirit, fixed his eyes on a crippled man who asked him for alms. Moved by the Holy Spirit, he told the crippled man that he did not have any money to give him, but he could give him what he had. And with authority in the kingdom and power in the name of Jesus, he grabbed the crippled man's hand, lifted him up, and told him to rise up and walk. Immediately, the crippled man who hadn't walked for over forty years was instantly healed.

This was a miracle! He had been there forty-plus years. All those who worshipped at that temple must have seen him and known him. The crippled man then followed Peter and John, walking and praising God for what He had done. Imagine this scene: Peter and John walking into the temple, and this guy who was crippled was now jumping and praising God, clinging to Peter and John, and making a raucous. This must have gotten everyone's attention. Hearing this guy, they were probably wondering what was going on. The crowd must have been running to see this, and then after witnessing this they must have told others what had happened—a domino effect. Then next thing Peter knows is that he has an instant need to preach the gospel. He told them that this man who was crippled was healed by the power of God and by faith in the name of Jesus, the one they crucified and was raised by God from the dead. In the middle of Peter's preaching, the priests had the temple guards arrest Peter. Acts records that about five-thousand men believed the message that day. Can you imagine the domino effect of people running to see what happened when five-thousand believed!

After the guards arrested Peter and John, they stayed in jail overnight. The next day, the high priest asked Peter, "By what power or by what name did you do this?" Peter told him in no uncertain terms, "It was by the name of Jesus, the one YOU crucified, and whom God raised from the dead, and through faith in Jesus' name this man was made whole."

Acts 4:13 records the following:

> Now as they observed the confidence of Peter and John and understood that they were uneducated and untrained men, they were amazed, and began to recognize them as having been with Jesus.

When Peter and John were released, they went to all their companions and prayed. We read this in Acts 4:29 -31:

> "And now, Lord, take note of their threats, and grant that Your bond-servants may speak Your word with all

> confidence, while You extend Your hand to heal, and signs and wonders take place through the name of Your holy servant Jesus." and when they had prayed, the place where they had gathered together was shaken, and they were all filled with the Holy Spirit and began to speak the word of God with boldness.

Well, that is what happened—all of Jerusalem was disrupted! There was so much authority and power coming from Peter.

> And all the more believers in the Lord, multitudes of men and women, were constantly added to their number, to such an extent that they even carried the sick out into the streets and laid them on cots and pallets, so that when Peter came by at least his shadow might fall on any one of them. Also, the people from the cities in the vicinity of Jerusalem were coming together, bringing people who were sick or afflicted with unclean spirits, and they were all being healed (Acts 5:14-16).

Peter continues preaching the gospel, is imprisoned, is let out by an angel, gets pulled before the Pharisees again. Here he tells them that he cannot obey them, but will obey God only. Peter is totally disrupting the world around him with the power and authority of the kingdom. In Acts 8, we see Philip going down to Samaria to preach the gospel, healing the sick, and casting out evil spirits. When it was heard by the Jerusalem church that Samaria had received the gospel, they sent Peter and John. They were laying hands on them so they could receive the baptism of the Holy Spirit, just like they did on the day of Pentecost.

Early in Acts 9, Saul is converted and starts his apostleship path as Paul. Later in Acts 9, Peter preaches through the region, heals the sick, and ends up raising Tabitha from the dead. In Acts 10, Peter is used as a leader and transitional figure in the second great move of the Holy Spirit. The first great move was the outpouring of the Holy Spirit in Jerusalem, Judea, and Samaria, in which Peter was a key leader along with the rest of the apostles. But the second move is a major transition for the Jewish world, the outpouring of the Spirit among the Gentiles, where Paul is to carry this torch and authority to bring this message.

Acts 10 tells the story of Cornelius, an Italian centurion, who was a Roman. According to tradition, these were two strikes against him. He was not only a Gentile, but a centurion who commanded Roman troops. Most centurions oppressed and held the Jews and submitted people to Rome. Cornelius was a devout man and had a hunger for God. He was kind and charitable to the Jewish people, probably unlike most centurions. One day when Cornelius was praying, he had a vision. In the vision, an angel told him to call for Peter. The angel told him where Peter was and with whom he was staying. Cornelius immediately sent for Peter.

Before Cornelius's servants arrived for Peter, Peter had a vision. God set a table and prepared Peter for the next work. In the vision, God showed Peter that what He made clean is clean. Through this vision, Peter was realizing that the Gentile nations would be fellow heirs to the kingdom of God.

When Cornelius's servants met Peter, they told him that Cornelius had a vision and hence sent for him. Peter and his associates then went to Cornelius's house. Cornelius invited his close friends and relatives and waited for Peter to arrive. When Peter arrived at Cornelius's house, he told them of his vision and how through it, God prepared him to preach to them, and that God calls them holy as He calls the Jews holy. Peter preached the gospel there. During his preaching, their hunger was so great. God was so excited to give them the Holy Spirit that the Holy Spirit fell on them as it did on the day of Pentecost. Right during Peter's preaching—bam! The Holy Spirit hit them. How did they know it was the Spirit? Because they heard them speaking in tongues.

Peter reported back to Jerusalem about what had happened, and this set the table for Paul to step up into his ministry. Peter was primarily sent to the Jews as an unlearned Jew. Paul was primarily sent to the Gentiles as a highly-learned Jew. It's amazing how God jumbles things up!

The first great move of the Holy Spirit (revival) was to the Jews; the second was to the Gentiles. Peter was a main figure in the first and a transitory leader in the second.

I have outlined all this to show how Peter learned and was transformed as a leader in the kingdom. He learned to walk in the authority of the Lion through the meekness of the Lamb. All these events show the authority he lived in. His process should be a great encouragement to all of us, because if we want to be a kingdom leader, we will have to go through similar transformation.

I can think of no better way than to take Peter's words and relate them back to his transformation and learning of how to be a powerful kingdom leader—a Kingdom Master Builder. These words were written towards the end of his life. So these truths were woven into his being and were important for him to communicate as he moved on to be with the Lord.

I would ask all who read this to make an ongoing prayer to the Lord to help you see the truths that are stated here, and help you walk in these truths. That you will have the grace to receive these truths, and that it will change and transform you into the leader God wants you to be. Pray that the Holy Spirit would change you where you need to adjust, give you grace to hear what He is saying, and transform you into a vessel who can walk in the authority of the Lion, as a result of the meekness of the Lamb living in you.

> Therefore, I exhort the elders among you, as your fellow elder and witness of the sufferings of Christ, and a partaker also of the glory that is to be revealed, shepherd (FEED) the flock of God among you, exercising oversight not under compulsion, but voluntarily, according to the will of God; and not for sordid gain, but with eagerness; nor yet as lording it over those allotted to your charge, but

proving to be examples to the flock. And when the Chief Shepherd appears, you will receive the unfading crown of glory. You younger men, likewise, be subject to your elders; and all of you, clothe yourselves with humility toward one another, for God is opposed to the proud, but gives grace to the humble. Therefore, humble yourselves under the mighty hand of God, that He may exalt you at the proper time (1 Peter 5:1-6).

When many commentators explain this section, they relate back to the historical significance of eldership among the Jewish community, which I am sure has some importance. But I want to relate it back to Peter's journey in his relationship with God and how that helped him learn about kingdom leadership. Remember Peter before his transformation—the guy who got a great commendation from Jesus about his confession of who He is with a statement of the authority that would-be available to him. He was rebuked by Jesus for thinking of his own self-interests before God's interests. Peter was vying for the highest position in the kingdom and boasting that although everyone else would deny Jesus, he would not. Then Peter denied Jesus and lived in despair with the burden of that denial and lost all that he sacrificed while walking with Jesus for three years. Jesus rises from the dead, restores Peter, and reaffirms his place in the kingdom and his role as a shepherd. Peter preached the first sermon after the Pentecostal outpouring. These sermons, with their recorded healings and miracles, are recorded in the book of Acts. I could go on, but hopefully that gives you the picture.

Peter has gone through all these things, been a leader in the kingdom for thirty-plus years, and is writing the above words. He says that our first duty is to feed the flock of God. He is using the same words Jesus spoke to him. The word *shepherd* also can be translated "feed" (Greek: *poimainō*), and means more to feed the flock with the necessary food, like to furnish a pasture for food. Jesus used this same word in John 21 when He was restoring and exhorting Peter to feed His sheep. The third time, in John 21 as well as in Peter's writings, he used a word that has a broader meaning (Greek: *bosko*). It not only refers to feeding, but more like acts of overseeing and to promote the overall spiritual welfare of the flock, which includes discipline, authority, restoration, and instruction to individuals and the church universally,

Peter directly goes into what is behind the willpower to do this, which speaks to motivation. Motivation to keep doing what we do is always important because it will govern the intricacies and the quality of our behavior. He first says it is not under compulsion. *Compulsion* literally means by force or constraint. The first part is that we are not forced by God to do this, even if we are called. We do this because it is our passion and calling. We do this because we love God. Because we love God we love His people, and what we do for His people is an overflow of our calling. This means that we are doing this as our vocation.

There are times when we know what the right thing to do is, and what we are called to do. But we do them grudgingly because we really don't want to do them. Then we must ask ourselves the question: "Why would that be?" I think generally we are drawn away by our own desire for other things. I think Jesus may refer to that as losing our first and most important love. It is so important to learn to maintain our love and interaction with God in an intimate and personal way. That will always influence everything else in the right direction.

Peter brings in an important topic when he tells us not to do this just for money or prestige. That does not mean that those who are elders should not be paid, or even well paid. It means that it is not the motivating factor. Somehow, when we do what we love to do, and we do it passionately with all our heart, the product of what we do is readily apparent to those around us as something valuable. People will invest in it.

Paul in his letter to Timothy says, "For the **love of money** is the root of all sorts of evil." It does not say that money is the root of all sorts of evil. Rather, the LOVE of money is. How many men and women of God have been sidetracked and derailed in their effectiveness in the kingdom by making decisions purely based on financial gain? We have discussed previously the difference between good and evil. Good causes you to make decisions for the benefit of others, even when it is at your own expense. Evil causes you to make decisions for your own benefit at the expense of others. Peter exhorts us to not do things just for money. As Paul states, it just brings many trials that don't need to happen and leads to our own spiritual ruin and destruction. One of the most slippery slopes that will rob us of authority as a spiritual leader in the kingdom is to have the love of money influence our decisions. May God have mercy on us and grant us grace not to fall into this trap of traps!

The last point is to not act just for the prestige of being a "spiritual leader." When we look for prestige and receive honor from men, it will lead us to all kinds of decisions that will be far from the will of God. Jesus said in John that you cannot believe if you receive honor (glory from one another). Meaning, if prestige and honor from man becomes more important to you than listening to things that God wants you to do, you will not have faith to believe. This is a very powerful statement! Again, it speaks to motives and the quality of what we do as being approved by God first and foremost.

Something happens to our spiritual understanding and barometer when we start liking the prestige and honor that comes from authority first rather than loving God. This leads us to make decisions that are in our best interest without considering the importance of other's interests.

I read a book about a great former spiritual leader of the nineteenth century, A.W. Tozer. He was known for his revelatory teachings, spiritual understanding, and oratory skills. He wrote something in one of his books that caught my attention. I am paraphrasing what he wrote. When the church service was over, he would never go out and greet people as they left. He did not want to get drawn in by their praise and start believing the things they may praise him for. He had an understanding that it could easily influence his motives in the wrong way.

I want to clarify that it is not wrong for us to greet people, but this person knew his weakness and was led of the Lord to not do it. We all need to look at our own hearts, listen to the Lord, and hear what He wants to tell each of us individually.

On a personal note, I distinctly remember teaching one Sunday morning when we had two services. In the first service, my preaching was hitting on all cylinders. I sensed that the people were being blessed and God was anointing every word. There was about thirty minutes between the two services. I stepped off the stage, started talking to a few people, and asked a few leading questions about the sermon, looking for feedback. I t heard a voice on the inside of me questioning why I was asking for feedback. Again it spoke, "You are just looking for their praise. Go sit in the office and rest and wait for the next service." Oops! I think God located me. It wasn't that honest feedback wasn't important, but my motives were a bit off. I was just wanting to hear praise from men. Somehow I didn't even hear the response from the people of whom I asked the question because the Lord was having this internal conversation with me.

Peter goes into making another exhortation in verse 3, "Not lording it over those allotted to your charge but be an example to the flock." This means that you are not the king who controls everybody. Even though we may be a leader, elder, pastor, or bishop. Whatever title or spiritual office we hold does not give us the authority to control and manipulate people.

I see this especially as a danger for spiritual leaders. We tend to couch things in spiritual terms like "God said," or "I am the spiritual leader, and you need to obey me." As leaders we can often be deceived by our own importance. Just because God uses us in some way, and we have revelation and anointing, we think that we are more important than we are. Any leader who thinks that he knows the will of God for all the people under his care is treading on shaky ground. Yes, God gives you a position from which to care for them and wisdom to help them. But in helping them, you need to hold them with a soft open grip and allow them to do what they want to do—good or bad. That is just the way God does it.

Leadership is about influencing people, not controlling people. If we must tell people that we are the leader or pastor or apostle, and by that you have authority, then your authority is man-made, and man attained. If you are the leader, you don't need to tell anybody. It is apparent to everyone.

Remember in the introduction I said kingdom leaders influence and intentionally guide and direct people toward behaviors, beliefs, and characteristics of God's kingdom and it is done with kingdom principles. A kingdom principle is a lifestyle that allows the authority that rests in the kingdom to work through us. When we walk in the principles of leadership outlined in this book, the authority of kingdom leadership will rest on us. The authority of the Lion will rest on those who walk in the meekness of the Lamb.

Peter is representing this principle when he goes on to talk about how the younger should submit in respect to the elders in authority. Submission is an honor and respect for the person, office, and calling. Peter goes on to say a wonderful thing, "Clothe yourself in humility, for God resists the proud and gives grace to the humble." Here is the subject of humility again. Humility is the virtue of virtues, principle of principles, and the key of keys which allows the precious authority of the kingdom to have its influence over us.

In the end, as a shepherd and leader, we want the Chief Shepherd to place on our heads that unfading crown of glory for being a faithful servant.

For those of you who want to influence the world around you, your family, friends, co-workers, towns, cities, states, and countries: If your desire is to receive the authority of the Lion, learn to walk in the kingdom principles of the meekness of the Lamb. For the Lamb was worthy to receive glory, honor, and power!

# ABOUT THE AUTHOR

Scott was ordained in 1985 and has worked in various ministerial roles in churches and other Christian organizations for the past thirty plus years—leading, teaching, organizing, and training believers in the kingdom of God. Scott has operated in various five-fold ministries and has a strong prophetic, teaching and healing anointing, often challenging people to know God and fulfill their God-ordained destiny. He has written many prophetic teachings and courses such as *Understanding Divine Healing through The Ministry of Jesus*; *Paul's Spiritual Secret*; *Revival*; *Kingdom Leadership and Authority*; *Prayer, His Presence, and Intimacy with God*; *The Person, Gifts, and Ministries of the Holy Spirit;* and *Releasing the Power of the Heart and The Soldier of Christ*. Scott is a pastor at Gateway Christian Fellowship in West Haven, and the founder of Kingdom Master Builders.

For additional information and teaching from Scott, please go to KingdomMasterBuilders.com, where many more of his teachings and other material can be obtained. Kingdom Master Builders is all about what is written in the book, building the Kingdom and dominion of God in the hearts and minds of mankind. If interested in contacting Scott for Ministry opportunities, please email him at Kingdommasterbuilders@gmail.com.

# OTHER BOOKS BY SCOTT TAVOLACCI

Understanding Divine Healing and the Ministry of Jesus

In 1991, the Lord spoke to me about studying His Word on divine healing. This caught me off guard. Not that I had the subject down pat, but had intensely studied the subject for numerous years, t I had taught numerous times on various ways of divine healing, read countless books on the subject, memorized almost every scripture on healing in the bible and listened to more local, national and international ministers on the subject than I can remember. This time, though, the Lord spoke to me and said I want you to study how I did it, and told me to study how *He* ministered divine healing to people. Since I read the Gospels more times than I can remember and read many of the accounts of Jesus ministering healing, I thought this would be a short study. Well, months later, I realized how ignorant I was (and probably still am.) It was one of the richest times I have had studying the subject of divine healing.

The heart of what I learned is that Jesus learned how to hear God the Father and do His will. Jesus said:

> "I tell you the truth, the Son can do nothing by himself. He does only what he sees the Father doing. Whatever the Father does, the Son also does. For the Father loves the Son and shows Him everything He is doing. In fact, the Father will show Him how to do even greater works than healing this man. Then you will truly be astonished" (John 5:19-20 NLT).

Jesus spoke this as a result of the Pharisees and religious leaders questioning Him on why He healed a paralytic man on the Sabbath. It's a question we also seem to ask ourselves: why Jesus did things the way He did. The New Testament shows a great diversity of ways He ministered to people—thus, there are a great may reasons why He did things the way He did. Too often we try to minister healing to people through a formula of faith, or the theory that physical healing is a result of some inner healing that needs to take place first, before divine healing can be manifested. Although both schools of thought have a great amount of truth to them, we can't rely or have faith in a formula that someone else understands.

We need a personal revelation of Jesus the Healer. We need to rely on God and hear how God wants us to minister to each individual. What I realized is that there is no one formula to divine healing. Sure, we need to understand principles of faith; sure, we need to understand the power and authority in the name of Jesus; sure, we need to understand how to lay hands on the sick; sure, we need to understand how to flow in the gifts of the Spirit. I could go on and mention different ways God manifests Himself. But what we need to ask is what God wants to do in each situation.

In this book I will endeavor to teach every principle of divine healing that I have learned. I will start in the place of relationship, seeking to understand how God can get people's hearts to engage with Him, so He can minister His healing power to them. Jesus always endeavored to do what He saw His Father do. Although man may not understand God's ways, God the Father always had specific purposes in what and how He did things. If we can understand the heart of the Father, we will come to a greater understanding of why God wants to heal, the various ways He heals and, most importantly, how He tries to engage people's hearts on an intimate level, so they can receive from Him.

www.ingramcontent.com/pod-product-compliance
Lightning Source LLC
Chambersburg PA
CBHW052025070526
44584CB00016B/1909